Marcia Mastach

D0852272

THE CREWEL NEEDLEPOINT WORLD
Barbara H. Donnelly **Karl W. Gullers**

THE CREWEL NEEDLEPOINT WORLD

by Barbara H. Donnelly
Photography by Karl W. Gullers

Gullers International, Inc.
New York, Stockholm, Copenhagen

Morgan and Morgan, Inc.
Dobbs Ferry, New York

To
Bucky King, who taught me
Virginia Phillips, who pushed me
Karl Gullers, who inspired me

Copyright © 1973 Barbara Donnelly and Karl Gullers
Library of Congress Catalog Card Number: 73-80438
ISBN: 0-87100-041-5
All rights reserved
Printed in Sweden
by Ljungföretagen, Örebro
Typography: Ulf Hedenäs

The Crewel Needlepoint World

As a needlework designer and teacher, I have been aware of the need for a simple yet comprehensive book for the beginner in my field of needlepoint and crewel.

At last the time came when I could sit down and write this book. I had, by the best of good luck, the finest photographer in the world to help me, some powerfully talented students' and friends' work to use, and an understanding family who went along with me.

With the thought always in mind of the person who has never held a needle in her hand, I have tried to remember all the different problems that my beginners faced and dealt with successfully, and to give you the benefit of all of our learning experiences. You see, I found that teachers learn from their students as much as students learn from the teacher. I thank my students one and all.

Sometimes the student is helped by remembering a little rhyme, or memorizing a phrase to do a stitch with ease, or even by the teacher telling her; "Relax, go at your own speed no one is testing you at the end."

Remember, THIS IS FOR FUN. It's a great hobby, one that is inexpensive when compared with the time spent. You can carry it with you; you do not have to go to it. It is not messy to work with, and it gives great pleasure to others in years to come.

Whether you use this book from start to finish, or pick sections to read that will help you solve a particular problem, I hope you will be inspired to go on and learn more about the art of crewel and needlepoint and try doing your own designs.

We all need the satisfaction of creating with our own two hands in this mechanized age. If you follow the guidelines set down throughout this book, you too will know the feeling of accomplishment and satisfaction that needlewomen have when people say, "Did you create this? It's beautiful."

The beginner might start by doing her first piece in diagonal tent as this one was done. (See page 64.)

This sampler, dated 1846, proves that "flame stitch" or "Florentine" is nothing new.

Keep your eyes open and see the many designs around you. Look for design in tree branches, flowers and all nature. Also look at magazines, fabrics, woodcuts, paintings, etc.

"I Can't Draw a Straight Line"

It is such an old cliché, and yet ask any ten people how they feel about designing their own needlepoint or crewel and they will come out with that line.

There is a mystique about the word "design," perpetuated by I know not whom, but which certainly exists. You would think you had to go to the Pratt Institute in New York, or the Art Institute of Chicago, and have your work hung in the Louvre in Paris before you should sit down and do some designing on your own.

If this book does nothing else, I hope it lays that feeling or delusion to rest for all time as far as you are concerned. Designing is nothing sacred, something to be used only by the chosen few. The principles governing it have been laid down for hundreds of years. I hope to translate them into non-technical language for the uninitiated, just as I have done for many years in my classes.

If you follow these principles, and the procedures you shall see in pictures in this book, it should be as easy as reading a recipe in a good cookbook. (I might add I find cooking much harder than designing because the timing in cooking is so important.) Design you can take your time with, change everything around to suit yourself, down to the last stitch or line. I think it is remarkable that people will pay many dollars for something that is so easy to do oneself.

When I first wanted to design a piece of needlepoint, I went to a shop and was aghast at the price charged to put a design from a book about rugs on canvas. I had no idea how to proceed myself so I had to pay the price. This probably forced me into making the decision that I would learn to do it myself.

Later, I learned that it is time that costs and if you have that, you don't need to be Michaelangelo.

I am not going to suggest for one moment that you are going to turn into full-fledged artists who can use perspective, shade, and blend colors just by reading this book. What I do propose to show you are some shortcuts for translating your ideas from existing design to canvas or crewel. It isn't all that difficult.

Picture opposite page:
With diagonal tent you must take the precaution of looking at the warp (vertical), and weft (horizontal), of the canvas and go down the ladder covering the vertical intersection and come up the ladder covering the horizontal section of the canvas. This is vital so you don't have two rows going in the same direction and cause a line to form which will always show. See page 64 for further detail about this.

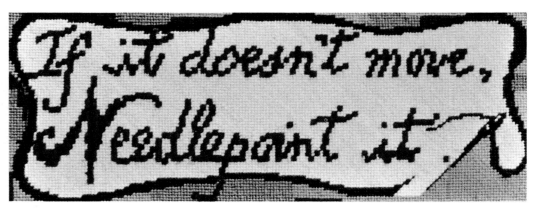

113 Suggestions of Things to Make

For the House

Pillow
Chair Seat
Bellpull
Trivet
Stair Treads
Rug
Fly Swatter Back
Picture
Luggage Straps
Tray Holder
Footstool
Clock Face
Chess Board
Door Pusher (under glass)
Paperweight
Table (under glass)

Coasters
Blotter Sides or Edges
Book Ends
Wallhanging
Headboard on Bed
Valance
Curtain Ties
Napkin Ring Holder
Screen Divider
Shutters
Tissue Box
Door Stop
Piano Bench
Christmas Tree Top
Christmas Tree Ornament
Christmas Stocking
Stock and Bond Portfolio
Flowerpot Cover
Bridge Table Cover
Wastebasket
Yardstick Cover
Toilet Seat Cover
Bolster
Ice Bucket Cover
Stereo Amplifier Cover
Toaster Cover
Teapot Cover
Typewriter Cover

For Men and (or) Women

Pockets on Clothes
License Plate (only
    state or country where
    one license required)
Passport Folder
Stationery Holder
Vest
Slippers
Belt
Suspenders
Guitar Strap
Book Mark
Buttons
Golf Club Covers
Tennis Racket Cover
Flask Case
Ski Cover
Gun Case Cover
Fishing Rod Cover
Tennis Ball Can Cover
Violin Case Cover
Wheel and Binnacle
Cover for Boats
Binocular Case
Camera Case
Bowling Ball Case
Compass Case

For Women

Shoes
Needlecase
Jewel Box
Purse
Keychain
Pincushion
Cigarette Case
Lighter Case
Hat
Luggage Name Tag

Meeting Name Tag
Choker
Hairband
Cuff and Collar Set
Coat
Wallet
Wig Case Cover
Tote Bag
Shoe Buckles
Watchband
Chatelaine
Rain Hat Case
Scissors Case
Cosmetic Case
Credit Card Holder
Pin
Travel Pill Case

For Children

Toy Box Cover
Miniature Chair Seat
Toys
Doll
Barrette

For Men

Cummerbund for Tuxedo
Tobacco Pouch
Pipe Cover
Tie

For Dogs or Cats

Coat
Collar
Snow Boots

Steps to Take	Suggestions
First Step For whom is it intended?	House, Yourself, Friend, Family, Child, Church or Synagogue.
Second Step What are you going to make?	Complete list on opposite page. You may have more ideas of your own to add.
Third Step Where is it to be placed or worn?	Look around room to decide what room will take: may a stripe or pattern, etc., be used? What is needed to complement the room? Scale can be very important here. Do you want piece you make to blend or dominate?
Fourth Step What colors should I use?	Person: His or her color choice should be considered. If for yourself, you already know what colors you wear best. Place: The colors already in use in the room should normally be chosen unless you want to add an accent color.
Fifth Step Do you want to use traditional, modern, or what?	Naturally, one wouldn't put a Peter Max poster with a Chippendale setting. Choose something in keeping with the style already established. Picking up a design that already exists in room can unite the whole.
Sixth Step Do your research first.	It is worth the time to look it up so that after a year's work someone doesn't take great glee in pointing out its faults. In other words, don't put an abstract on a William and Mary chair.
Seventh Step Decide on Measurements	Pillow: Should it be 10″×10″, 12″×14″, 14″×14″, or 12″×20″? Chair Seat: Have upholsterer make pattern in muslin. Do not let him talk you into a square or rectangle to work. Belt: Measure carefully, then add 1″ to length.
Eighth Step What size canvas do I want and how much should I buy?	Always buy two inches more all around your design than you will need. Canvas is sold by the number of threads to an inch. The more complicated the design, or the more shading you want, the more threads to the inch you must buy. Linen comes in loose weaves for surface stitchery and close weaves for traditional crewel work.
Ninth Step How do I put my design on canvas?	See section, Simple As "Paint By Number," page 24.

"Diaper patterns" are combinations of stitches. Try doing your own.

Personalize your purse with your initials by using leftover pieces of canvas.

Use up leftover yarn by making keychains and needlecases for friends.

This Ramsay Tartan footstool would probably wear about ten years in fabric, but one hundred or more in needlepoint.

Using the "theory of three," see page 77.

Read It—Do It

I have had women in my stichery classes who were terrified of trying to adapt a design for their own use but who, when they got in my design class and really approached the subject with an open mind, were amazed to find they could do it easily.

There is no special hocus pocus to it at all. It is simply a matter of first deciding some things about yourself or the one for whom you would like to make a piece of needlework, such as: what colors you or she likes, what you want to make, what subject or theme you want to use and where you want the piece to be placed or worn.

On pages 12 and 13 are diagrams to help you to see the basic points you will wish to cover in order to make a design.

Don't ever make the assumption that you don't know what you like or what colors attract you. Think back a moment. Is it not true that you have decided all your life what clothes you like, what hairstyle best suits you, what colors those clothes should be, what size handbag to buy, and the like? Think even further. Haven't you decided what apartment to rent, or house to buy, the furniture, the drapes, rugs, upholstery, etc. to go in it? You really have been making decisions about design all your life and that didn't seem too hard, now did it? In fact, it was FUN and this is too.

You have worked hard to achieve the right scale for the rooms you have. You have not put furniture that is too large for the size of the rooms in your house. You have usually found one piece of furniture to dominate the whole, and grouped your chairs and sofa for easy conversation, so that your eye is drawn to one place first, using the fireplace perhaps, as your focal point. These things you have done unconsciously using the seven principles of design. (See Conspiracy Seven) You have absorbed these points unbeknownst to yourself.

Go back to the diagram and list of things to make, then think again.

If the design is for someone else, take into consideration his or her hobbies. They may be sports such as hockey, football, sailing, golf, horseback riding, surfing, basketball, bowling, curling, soccer, bicycling, or archery to name a few. Think of the less active hobbies such as stamp collecting, antiques, knitting, painting, and reading. These can all be successfully depicted.

Now that the major questions of who, what, where, color, and size have been decided, let's go ahead!

CANVAS: Comes in white, beige or cream. If you are planning a Florentine pillow or plan on using any other straight stitch, I suggest the beige, otherwise the white is fine. It comes with single threads running horizontally and vertically (mono), or double threads running both ways (penelope). For purposes of this book, I am talking about mono or single thread canvas.

The reason I like mono canvas is that I prefer working on it, and think it is easier on the eyes. A good many stitches do not work well on penelope (double mesh) canvas. Only half cross stitch must be worked on penelope. Penelope is longer wearing though.

You want to find the shop that supplies the best French or Swiss canvas. There are all kinds of substitutes, but pick the canvas up yourself and study it. If you hold it against the light, and it isn't fuzzy, and doesn't feel rough to your hands, it is what you want. If there is fuzz between the holes, go somewhere else, since that is what causes your yarn to break.

THE SMALLER THE NUMBER, THE LARGER THE HOLES.

Example: Five mesh (quick point) is used for rugs, sixteen mesh for an eyeglass case where more detail is needed.

Generally, you will be using canvas ranging from 10 to 18 mesh per inch. I do use 24, 26, 28, and even 37 for petitpoint, but that requires a magnifying glass or else your eyes will swell shut after three days and you won't be able to see the newspaper. It happened to me.

Evenweave linen may also be used if you don't want to fill in the background but it won't wear as well.

LINEN TWILL: Long wearing and used mainly for traditional crewel work. Burlap, cotton, silk, and other materials may be used for the more modern surface stitchery we see today. I do not recommend felt. Otherwise, just about anything that can be washed and blocked may be used.

There are many yarns you can use, and you can achieve many different textures depending on whether the yarn is wool, silk, cotton, or any of numerous other materials. Practically anything that can be put through the eye of a needle and will bend can be used, even human hair.

Equipment You Will Need

Background Materials for Needlepoint

Materials for Crewel

Yarn for Needlepoint

As we are just beginning, let me tell you what I feel are the finest yarns made. They are Paternayan crewel and Persian yarns. I prefer the crewel as it isn't so fuzzy, has a tighter twist, and is a single strand of yarn. But I must admit most shops around the country use the Persian and they do have about forty more colors. Persian is longer wearing and, therefore, is better for rugs. The retail name is Paterna. If you can't find this, ask for any good tapestry, Persian, crewel, or needlepoint yarn, depending on your use. I don't recommend knitting wools as they break and do not wear well.

Yarn for Crewel

Appleton from England is my favorite yarn for traditional crewel. For surface stitchery which uses the same stitches but in a freer fashion or manner, one uses whatever seems to complement the background material and your design. Sometimes, for an example, you could use heavy string or even rope from the hardware store as a combination with other yarns on a rough heavy material. Again, experiment to find exactly the right combination of textures. As another example, on a fine piece of silk, only the fine Swiss silks would look appropriate. A rough yarn would look inappropriate.

Needles

Tapestry needles are large-eyed and blunt-tipped. They are used for needlepoint. The larger the number, the smaller the needle is. For most of your work #18 is best unless you're doing petit point. Most shops sell mixtures in one package so you might buy two packages, one containing only #18 and the other holding a variety.

For crewel use crewel needles. These have large eyes and sharp points. It is advisable to buy a variety pack with many sizes included. If using many weights of yarn, many kinds of needles can be employed. Just be sure the eye is large enough for the yarn but not too large. If it is too large it will leave a hole in the material.

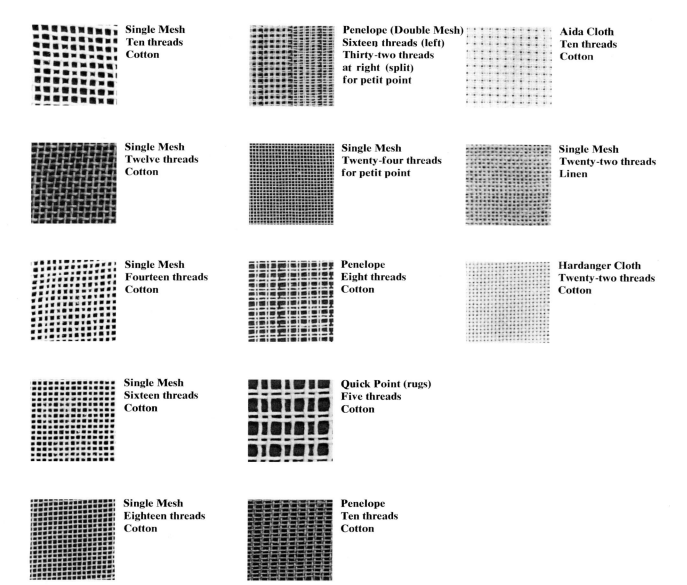

Single Mesh
Ten threads
Cotton

Penelope (Double Mesh)
Sixteen threads (left)
Thirty-two threads
at right (split)
for petit point

Aida Cloth
Ten threads
Cotton

Single Mesh
Twelve threads
Cotton

Single Mesh
Twenty-four threads
for petit point

Single Mesh
Twenty-two threads
Linen

Single Mesh
Fourteen threads
Cotton

Penelope
Eight threads
Cotton

Hardanger Cloth
Twenty-two threads
Cotton

Single Mesh
Sixteen threads
Cotton

Quick Point (rugs)
Five threads
Cotton

Single Mesh
Eighteen threads
Cotton

Penelope
Ten threads
Cotton

19

Simplify a busy fabric by taking only one major design from it. Duplicating the fabric exactly would have been overpowering.

Whimsy plays an important role in stitchery for children. Notice second boat is "an outhouse."

A modern sampler of family names done in crewel stitchery.

A rug done in diagonal tent with Swedish rya bees and fringe.

Simple as "Paint by Number"

For Canvas Work (Needlepoint)

There are several ways of going about painting your design on canvas or material but first let's talk about the design itself.

The person who wants to use a variety of stitches in a design must pick a design to adapt which has certain qualities.

First:
It must have areas large enough to show off the stitches chosen. Keep the design simple enough so the areas for each stitch are about 2″×2″.

Second:
Choose stitches on your working sketch so that they are not too "busy" or too many. (This is a common mistake. The beginner tends to use too many stitches and the design becomes lost.) This can be solved by keeping the number down to five or seven stitches at most as an "elegant sufficiency" and by keeping to a limited number of colors. If you want to do a sampler, go ahead with as many stitches as you want and tie the whole together by surrounding each stitch with the same color in perhaps tent stitch or Gobelin (page 78), or by sticking to three values of one color throughout, or even by three colors only, using a dark, light, and bright. See the bellpulls or wallhangings on page 41.

Third:
You must consider the wearing ability of the stitches you choose. If you are doing a wall hanging, any stitch may be used including many crewel stitches, but if it is for a footstool, chair, rug, etc., you must use stitches which are not so big that they don't wear well, or too raised so that they catch on things.

Fourth:
If one wants to translate an existing picture that has shading and you want to achieve the same effect, you MUST use one of the tent stitches.

Don't complain that you may have spent the last six months learning all the stitches of canvas work (needlepoint) and here I am putting you back to the tent stitch.

The reason is this: It is the smallest, most versatile stitch there is and don't ever let anyone tell you to drop it from your repertory. You can shade with other stitches like Swedish rya, the Gobelins, mosaic, etc., but this one is the best. To do an exact copy from some other medium to needlepoint with shading you must take this into account. I feel that diagonal tent is the one to use the most as it does not get your canvas out of shape nor do you have to keep turning your canvas.

These four requirements should be considered well before finally deciding on a design and stitches to use.

Buy your canvas in the size that will best suit your design.

Choosing the Right Size Canvas

If you don't need a lot of detail, buy ten or twelve threads to the inch. If it has a great amount of detail, buy fourteen, sixteen, or eighteen. For petit point use twenty-four as you get all the detail you want but this really should only be done under a magnifying glass. Even sixteen and eighteen can be hard on the eyes so take this into consideration too when buying.

You have chosen a design carefully, keeping in mind all the requirements mentioned, traced it onto a piece of paper the same size (see Increasing and Decreasing) as you want it to be on your canvas. Take a black felt tip marker and go over this design on your paper tracing to give you a good line to follow. NEVER USE MARKER ON SCRIM.

There are several ways to transfer this design to your canvas and I feel the non-artist should take the easiest route available.

Transferring Design to Canvas

Place your drawing on the table. Find the center and with a ruler draw down the whole center from top to bottom. Do the same with the horizontal center. This helps in lining up the design center with the canvas center.

Let us, for the sake of clarity, decide we are making a pillow that is going to be finished to the size of 14″×14″. We have bought a piece of canvas 18″×18″ or 1/4 yard. This is to assure us of two inches of unworked canvas all the way around. I can't overstress the necessity of this. It is heartbreaking to see a piece brought into my shop for finishing that has been worked up to the selvage edge. There is nothing in which to put your nails when blocking, and nothing for the finisher to use as a hem when making it into the finished piece.

The only alternative then to save the piece at all is to use some of the work on the margin of the hem. If the design should go out too far it is impossible to do even that, and you will need expert help to add canvas to all sides. (This is never really satisfactory.)

Glass Table Method

Finding the center of your scrim, which you have bound off with bias tape and hemmed on a sewing machine or by hand (or if time is of first importance, using masking tape), you run a sewing thread in and out down your center line and through center horizontally. This assures you that it will line up exactly with your center line of the design on paper. See picture of prepared canvas, opposite page.

Putting your design on paper face up on the table, place your canvas directly over it, pin together, and tape to table so it won't move around as you are painting.

Take a lamp, remove the shade, and place under the table. You will be able to see through the canvas perfectly to the design below.

Window Method

Prepare canvas and drawing the same way as in Table Method by drawing and sewing yarn horizontally and vertically through centers.

Tape drawing to a clean window against the sun. Tape the canvas that you have prepared over drawing lining up centers. Proceed as for Glass Table Method except, after outlining design, remove from window to fill in areas. Otherwise, you may end up with a bad backache.

TRUE CENTER

FALSE CENTER

Be sure to measure your designs with a ruler to find true center, and don't depend on your eyes. They can play you false. Run a thread through your canvas both horizontally and vertically so you may line up drawing exactly with canvas.

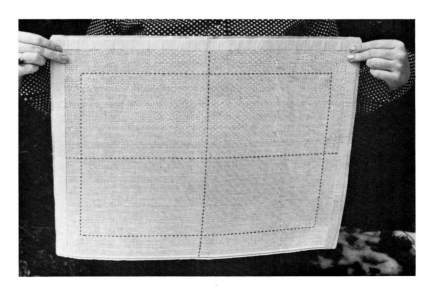

Painting Procedure

Put on old clothes that you don't care about.

NEVER, BUT NEVER, USE ANY KIND OF PEN ON CANVAS. I say this with the knowledge that someone will give me an argument, but I can't go along with the use of a pen or marker. I have seen too many pieces absolutely ruined by felt pens and the like. Use acrylic paint from tubes (not premixed). Do not use acrylic pens.

Purchase two eyedroppers from the drugstore. Drop some polymer medium, which is an additive, into the paint. (It comes in a jar at the art shop). Using this, apply a mixture of water, polymer medium, and acrylic paint to your scrim (canvas) in color desired. Use a good fine-pointed brush to outline first.

To mix the colors you will need, buy just enough to get started, and add colors later if you want a larger range.
See suggested Basic Paint Box.

You could also just buy a light shade of grey and paint in the outline or if you want to make your canvas look like a painting, buy colors in Basic Paint Box. Buy a small pointed brush that you can further taper to a point with manicure scissors. Also, buy one slightly larger for filling in.

Collect your old jar tops, or use old pill boxes, or baby jars for mixing. The jar tops are just deep enough for mixing small jobs, and the baby jars for big jobs if you are doing several canvases at once.

Acrylics are generally used as is or mixed with water. I find that just a few drops of water are needed. Don't forget your polymer medium which looks like thick cream. Drop about three drops into the mixture. Use the eyedroppers for these procedures, but wash out polymer medium immediately and don't let it dry in eyedropper.

One of my artists doesn't use water except to keep her brush wet. She just uses acrylic and polymer medium. This keeps the colors brighter and ensures not getting the canvas too wet, as happens once in a while with someone who is not used to mixing colors. The beginner has a tendency to use too much water and it will buckle the canvas.

Outline your whole design first. That is why we used the dark lines on the paper design. Having outlined, you can leave the spaces or fill in with appropriate color. It is best to fill in the colors if you are using white canvas so there will be less chance of canvas showing through.

Once you have gone this far, I'm pretty sure you have some paint on your blouse. Doesn't that make you feel like Picasso? The girls in my design class really get a thrill out of this part of the course. Most of them have never played around with paints before and it is stimulating.

Some of them have even taken it up as a pastime. Try it, no matter how shy you feel about it. It gives you a feeling of accomplishment that nothing else does. Color is fun to work with and we all respond to it.

Let your piece dry for at least an hour before starting to stitch. The piece shouldn't be washed (no matter how fast you finish it) for at least a month so the acrylics can set. It can never run.

To get the colors you want, see **Captivating Color** for mixtures.

CAUTION: Be sure to wash out brushes and eyedropper immediately after use.

Transferring Design for Crewel

Make two drawings of your design in size desired. One should have all detail showing, the other just major outlines.

Prewash and iron your fabric. Be sure the warp and weft are straight. Pin design with major outlines only over stretched-out fabric (right side up). Stretch it on embroidery hoop. Backstitch with **doubled** thread through fabric and lines of design on paper until all major outlines are covered.

Tear away paper carefully and you have the outline of design on fabric ready to work.

Use second design as pattern to follow with secondary lines and color filled in. In this procedure you can see that you can change your mind even at the last minute and it won't matter.

THIS METHOD MAY ALSO BE USED ON CANVAS IF YOU PREFER.

Putting your design under the canvas, tape canvas to window and paint outline with acrylics. Never use pens.

Putting a lamp, with shade removed, under a glass table is another way to get your design on canvas.

31

Here you can see the difference between perle cotton and wool.

Any shape may be filled with crewel or needlepoint stitches. Size of shapes must be in different proportions so it won't become monotonous. Also check spaces between shapes (your background).

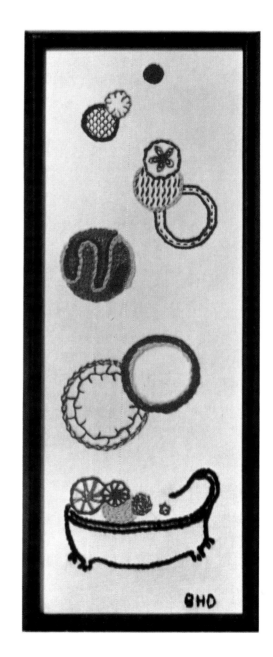

There's More Covered Than Tent Stitch

Continental Tent Versus Diagonal Tent Stitch

Continental tent has been the stitch taught for years in most department stores and shops as it is the fastest to teach. The big objection I have to it is simply that it pulls the canvas so out of shape that it sometimes takes four separate blockings to get it back to a ninety degree angle. My blocker and finisher says she wishes it had never been invented.

I like diagonal tent over continental. One of the reasons is that over the years that an heirloom is used, say on a chair seat, the rows of yarn done in continental won't break but the canvas between the rows WILL. This is not the case with diagonal tent. The interlocking diagonal rows make it impossible for the canvas to show and break. You also don't constantly have to turn your work upside down since diagonal is all done right side up. You can also jump around with your background with diagonal tent if you know the secret of watching the grain of the canvas.
(See diagonal tent diagram and description, page 64.)

Too Many Stitches?

I find the big fault with my students, is not that they don't learn the different stitches, but that they learn them too well. They know them and want to use them all in one piece of work. I enjoy all the stitches, more than 200 in canvas work and maybe a couple of thousand variations and stitches in crewel. I do not enjoy seeing them all at once in one piece of needlework. What happens is so confusing to the eye you don't see any of them but a blur of color and texture.

Unless you mean it to be a sampler such as St. George and the Dragon, (see cover) it is best to stay within the limits of five to seven stitches per piece.

As a matter of fact, some of the most attractive pieces are all done in one stitch and that one not necessarily being the tent stitch. I hope I'm not offending anyone who has thirty stitches on her latest piece. I just feel it is time to stop and look at what we are producing now. Let's not go overboard.

In this book I have attempted to give you what I feel are the most used of the stitches. Most others grow out of the ones I have diagrammed for you. Wherever possible I have used compensation in the diagrams to show you how to get over the hurdle of using stitches in odd shapes.

If you decide you'd like to try the bellpull or wallhanging as your first project in needlepoint, and follow the directions and the stitches is the order given, you will find the numbering and stitches tend to help you one with the other. For an example, if you do Smyrna first, and then you come to rice stitch, you can see that the two bases are the same. If you do flat stitch first, the mosaic stitch is just a smaller version.

Naturally, each stitch has complete directions but I feel it is a good way to start and you'll end up with a showpiece to hang on the wall and use for future reference when you're looking for just the right stitch to use in a certain place.

I have also included instructions for a belt in two stitches for a less time-consuming project that you can do, wash and block, finish, and be wearing in a week.

Following are diagrams and definitions to help you understand the words used frequently in the instructions.

The Sampler Bellpull or Wallhanging

Definitions

COMPENSATE: To shorten or lengthen a stitch to make it fit within an area. (See diagram for Diamond Eyelet Stitch or Slanted Gobelin Stitch.)

COMPOSITE STITCH: One process or stitch is done, then another process or stitch is done over the first. (Very often in two colors, see Rice Stitch.)

DIAPER PATTERN: A combination of stitches used together to form a pleasant design. (See Florentine Belt.)

SCOOP: A term meaning that once you have come to the front of the canvas from the back with your yarn to start your stitchery, you bend the canvas so the needle goes through the front to the back and comes out in front with the point all in one motion, and pulls through on the front keeping your right hand on front of canvas. (See diagram for diagonal tent stitch.)

UP AND DOWN THE LADDER: Going in steps up or down the canvas with the stitches usually on the diagonal from top left to bottom right (see Moorish Stitch and Diagonal Tent) or moving up & down along a Row (see Florentine Stitch).

WARP: The vertical thread of the canvas. (Or even weave material.)

WEFT: The horizontal thread of the canvas or material.

THREAD: Used here as a term for the warp and weft of canvas.

YARN: Used here as a term for the wool, cotton, silk etc. placed on canvas or material.

CANVAS WORK: The correct name for needlepoint. The word "needlepoint" is used mainly in the U.S. In other countries needlepoint is a lace.

Shortcuts

1. Never knot your yarn. Come up from back leaving one inch in back and work your stitches over the end. When you are down to about four inches of yarn, take needle to back of canvas and work the end of your yarn through stitches on the back for about an inch and cut off remainder.

2. Most yarn is precut when you buy it, but if yours is not, be sure the length is not over twenty inches as you'll wear it and your arm out with a longer one. Note: If using knitting yarn, make it ten inches as it has a looser twist than regular needlepoint yarn. I do not recommend knitting yarn.

3. Whenever possible I have numbered from left to right. I have taught it this way for years and for a simple reason. Our brains and eyes have been trained to follow from left to right in reading. It is also true that in cursive writing we have been used to going from bottom to top. You will find both these things true of my numbering and lettering wherever possible.

4. The first color used for each stitch is numbered. The second color used is lettered. Most of the stitches can be done in one or two or more colors depending on your design.

It is better to break up your design by separating the multicolor or two color stitches with one color stitches when using a combination of stitches.

5. Most stitches can be turned upside down to go back to do the next row and you will use the same numbers or letters. (Exceptions are diagonal tent, buttonhole, and Swedish rya.)

6. When using these stitches in forms other than squares or rectangles, it is better to start in the middle of the shape and work down, then turn

your work upside down and finish the shape. In this way you know when to compensate your stitches to fit the uneven area. See diagram.

7. To compensate a stitch you must shorten (the most usual way) or lengthen it to fit within the given area but keeping as much of the original stitch as possible. Sometimes it works out perfectly if you do 1/4, 1/2, or 3/4 of the stitch.

8. I have kept most of the stitches over a count of four horizontal threads of the canvas. Many of the stitches can be done over other counts like two, three, or five. Anything over six usually gets too big and doesn't wear well.

9. In the diagrams, I have deliberately showed compensation where I could. This gives you a better idea of how to do compensation than just hearing a definition. All compensation in diagrams has been marked with a cross within a circle to tell you it isn't the whole or complete stitch.

10. When you have to go more than 1/2 inch on the back of canvas, run yarn through worked stitches on back.

11. Always tie up your yarn after pulling threads out so yarn does not become tangled.

12. If you have never done canvas work or crewel, it is wise to learn to use a thimble on your middle finger.

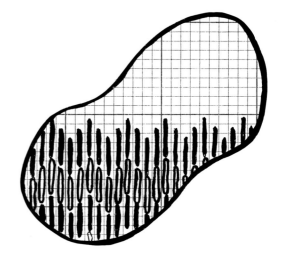

Directions for Florentine, Flame, or Bargello Belt

What To Buy:

1/8 yard of mono canvas 36″ wide in white or preferably beige. 12 threads to the inch.

One ounce of green (or any color you desire) in Paternayan Crewel or Persian Wool.

Three shades of blue, one ounce each (or any color you desire).

Number 18 needles.

Masking tape (not needed if you are hemming your canvas by hand or sewing machine).

A two inch buckle (one that has two sides which fasten together).

1/8 yard of material of your choice matching one of the colors you have chosen.

How to Start:

First bind off your canvas with masking tape using half the tape for each side and folding it over so the canvas will not fray as you work, or hem all sides. Measure your waist to know the exact length you want but adding one inch for finishing.

Thread your needle with three strands of crewel or two strands of Persian with lightest shade.

FLORENTINE STITCH is done as you write, from bottom to top, left to right. Starting up at one at center of canvas left, scoop your needle between two and three, four and five, etc. until you reach number 32 on your diagram. Turn your belt around and return finishing at 54. The next rows simply follow the first row set.

DIAMOND EYELET STITCH (center). See page 50.

WASHING, BLOCKING, AND FINISHING

When you have finished your needlepoint to the length you want, if you have not hemmed and used masking tape, you must at this point hem the unworked canvas on a sewing machine or by hand so that when you wash it, the unworked canvas will not unravel. See washing and blocking in **It's Indelible But It Ran.**

After cutting your fabric down to four inches by whatever your length plus two inches, turn your fabric and needlepoint together (right sides touching) and baste together. Run up the two long sides on sewing machine or by hand. Turn right side out, and apply belt buckle.

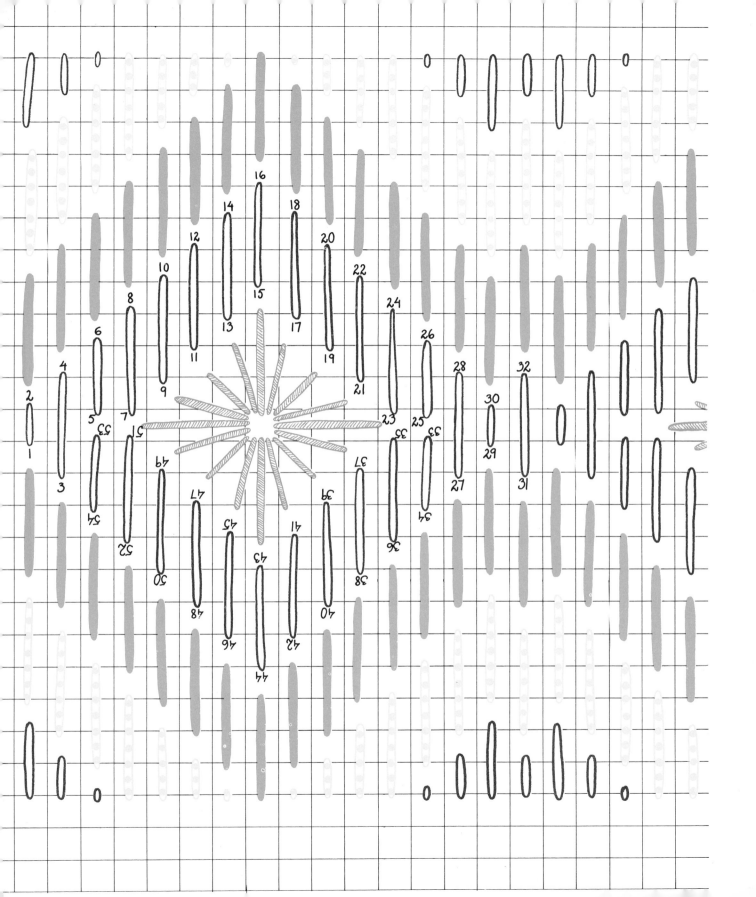

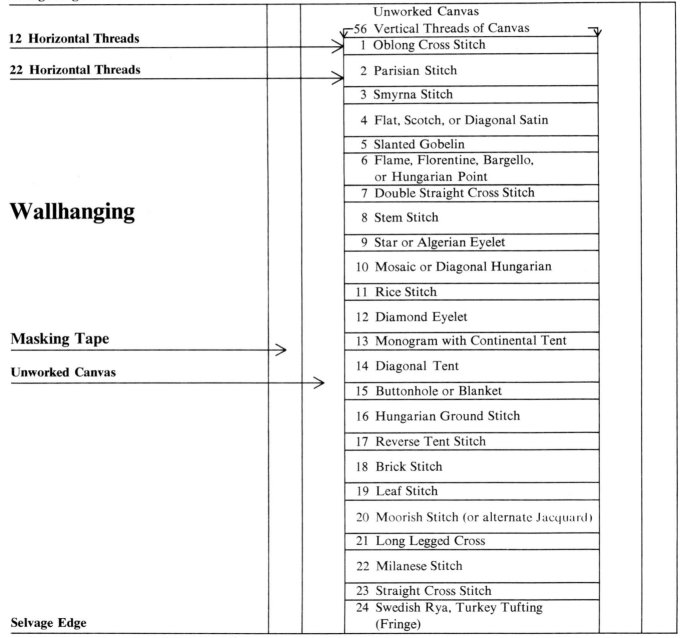

Selvage Edge

12 Horizontal Threads

22 Horizontal Threads

Wallhanging

Masking Tape

Unworked Canvas

Unworked Canvas
56 Vertical Threads of Canvas
1 Oblong Cross Stitch
2 Parisian Stitch
3 Smyrna Stitch
4 Flat, Scotch, or Diagonal Satin
5 Slanted Gobelin
6 Flame, Florentine, Bargello, or Hungarian Point
7 Double Straight Cross Stitch
8 Stem Stitch
9 Star or Algerian Eyelet
10 Mosaic or Diagonal Hungarian
11 Rice Stitch
12 Diamond Eyelet
13 Monogram with Continental Tent
14 Diagonal Tent
15 Buttonhole or Blanket
16 Hungarian Ground Stitch
17 Reverse Tent Stitch
18 Brick Stitch
19 Leaf Stitch
20 Moorish Stitch (or alternate Jacquard)
21 Long Legged Cross
22 Milanese Stitch
23 Straight Cross Stitch
24 Swedish Rya, Turkey Tufting (Fringe)

Selvage Edge

Wallhanging or Bellpull
Equipment Needed

To Start:

1/2 yard of beige or white mono (single mesh) French canvas. Beige is preferred as canvas is less likely to show through. Ask for 12 threads to the inch. Hold canvas up to light and be sure no fuzz shows between squares as this shows it is inferior canvas.

Choose three colors that will blend with the room in which it is to hang. Choose a light color, a dark color, and a bright color.

Get two ounces of each of the three colors.

#18 tapestry needles (These have blunt heads)

1" wide masking tape

Graph paper for lettering (one sheet)

One tube of acrylic paint in the lightest shade that you are using

One brush with fine point

To Finish:

1/4 yard (9"×36") velveteen in color to match colors chosen for sampler.

2 ice cream sticks

One drapery ring 7/8" and three drapery weights.

Nails, hammer, and board for blocking (40"×24").

Woolite (trade name for cold water detergent).

Preparing the Canvas

Using the masking tape and canvas, bind both raw sides with the tape by putting 1/2 inch of tape lengthwise on canvas and folding other 1/2" of tape around to other side covering raw edge.

Squeeze about one inch of acrylic paint into clean jar top and add a little water.

Paint Lines on Canvas as Follows

1. With the canvas in position where the long side is vertical, start in one inch from tape on left side and paint thread from top to bottom.

2. Counting the first painted line as one, count to the right (vertical threads) and paint 56th thread from top to bottom.

3. From selvage edge count down 8 regular threads and paint 8th horizontal thread between two already painted vertical lines.

4. Counting horizontal thread just painted as one, count down twelve threads and paint it between two vertical lines.

5. Counting next horizontal unpainted thread as one, count down twenty-two horizontal threads and paint it.

6. Alternate 4 and 5 rectangles until you have twenty-four rectangles. Note: Last rectangle will be much shorter than twenty-two threads. This is where the fringe goes.

Let dry two hours and you are ready to start doing your wallhanging sampler.

You do not thread a needle with yarn the same way as you do with thread. Put needle in left hand holding it by pointed end. Fold yarn over needle so it is doubled.

Hold yarn and needle at same time between right index finger and thumb so yarn doesn't show between them. Then pinch and slide yarn off needle.

Put needle (with eye towards yarn) between finger and thumb which is still pinching yarn. Release finger and thumb with a forward upward movement and yarn pops through eye of needle.

Note: This takes a little practice but is well worth it as it saves so much time later.

Threading a Needle with Yarn

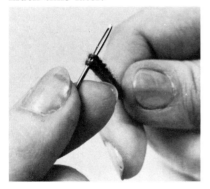
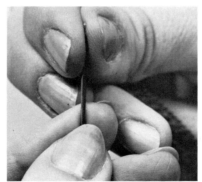

How to do the Stitches

1. Oblong Cross Stitch

Worked over 4 horizontal and 2 vertical threads of canvas. Crossed stitches must all be crossed in same direction. Coming up from back of canvas at one, hold about an inch of yarn on back of canvas and work your stitches over this yarn to hold it in the following manner. Scoop from two to three, four to five, etc. by keeping your right hand on the front of canvas. Turn at end of row upside down and do the same count to go back. If you run out of yarn, take needle to back of canvas and run about an inch of yarn through the yarn on back and snip of remainder. Start new thread by running through the same way on back of worked stitches and bringing to front at next number. (This stitch may also be done over three, five, six horizontal threads.)

For Wallhanging
Use three strands (or Ply) of yarn in your needle.
Start down below the fourth painted line on outside of left painted line and continue to right until you cover the 56th painted line on right. Turn upside down and continue with same count as before until you have three lines finished. This first stitch should be done in the color you want to separate the other two colors in the big rectangles. (Use this color in all small rectangles.)

2. Parisian Stitch

Work straight up and down over two and then four horizontal threads. (Turn work slightly after you start for greater ease in scooping.) Second row fits into first row over four and then two horizontal threads.

For Wallhanging
Use three-ply in your needle and second color. Starting outside painted line on left side, do the stitch until you reach outside the right hand painted line. Hold your second color by running needle through canvas outside design and winding up excess yarn until it is out of your way. Take another needle and start second row with third color and hold it at end of row. Now for third row, turn upside down and return with first color used in this rectangle. Alternate colors all the way down but do not cover next horizontal painted line.

Possible Uses
Background in one color or in two colors as stripes for sweater on person or any place where horizontal stripes are needed.

3. Smyrna

Composite Stitch: Worked over four horizontal and four vertical threads with bottom exactly like oblong cross stitch except wider. Top is bottom to top, left to right over four horizontal and four vertical threads.

For Wallhanging
Use three threads on first process (bottom), and three threads on top in second process. Bottom should be one of colors used in large rectangle and top color should be color used in small rectangle in #one.

Possible Uses
Border or Frame.
In two colors pretty as eyeglass or needle case.

IMPORTANT TO REMEMBER FOR WALLHANGING
Stitches in small rectangles cover top and bottom painted horizontal lines.
Stitches in big rectangles DO NOT cover top and bottom painted horizontal lines.

44

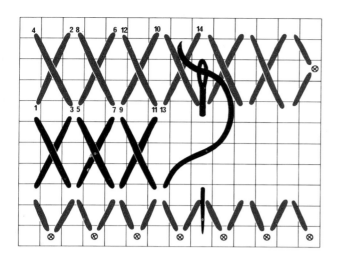

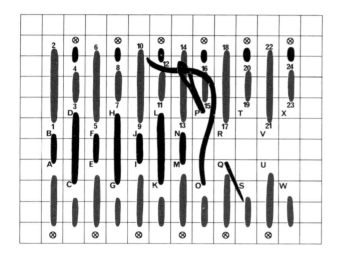

4. Flat, Scotch, or Diagonal Satin

Worked diagonally from left to right (not in straight rows as previous stitches), in groups of stitches making squares. Composed of slanted gobelin stitches starting with a tent stitch and ending with a tent stitch. Caution: Between #14 and #15 (between squares) straighten needle vertically and go under two horizontal threads. When you have done as many squares as you can to fill the space hold yarn, take second or third color as the case may be, and turn canvas sideways and using same count, work stitch same as before.

For Wallhanging
Use two-ply. Start outside left hand painted line down one horizontal thread.

You probably will have to compensate at the bottom of rectangle so check diagram and definitions for compensation.

Possible Uses
Wherever squares are needed.

5. Slanted Gobelin

Started with two tent stitches one over the other as compensation. Worked over four horizontal and two vertical threads. Ended with two tent stitches to fill in line.

For Wallhanging
Use three-ply. Small rectangle. Use first color.

Possible Uses
As drawers on chest or dresser or wherever rows of color are needed.

6. Flame, Florentine, Bargello or Hungarian Point

This stitch can be done in many ways with many variations. Usually you set the design with the first row with all rows following the first one only changing colors or shades or both. It is always a straight up and down stitch and usually progresses up and down the row like a flame. It may also meet and form a center diamond or medallion. The simplest version does not meet and we will use it here. Many books have been written on this one stitch and its variations.

For Wallhanging
Use three-ply. Large rectangle.

Possible Uses
Wonderful fast stitch for chair seats, pillows, etc.
In a stylized design may be used as water.

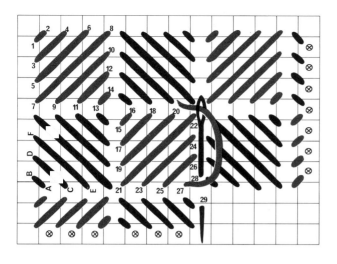

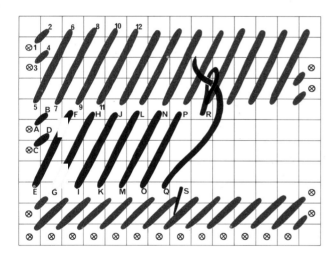

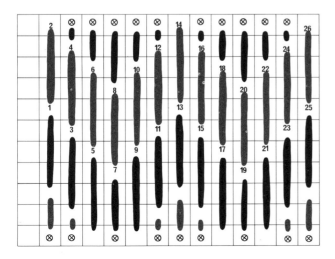

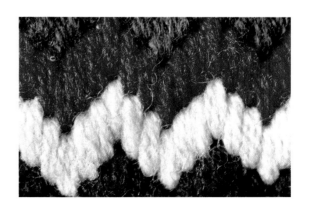

7. Double Straight Cross Stitch

Composite Stitch

Bottom: Over a count of four horizontal and four vertical threads forming an upright or Christian cross. Started from bottom to top and left to right.

Top: Over a count of two horizontal and two vertical threads forming a regular cross stitch. Start at bottom left of first stitch, scoop from two to three, and four to five, etc.

Notice that rows fit between each other.

For Wallhanging

Use three-ply on bottom and two on top using second color on bottom and first color on top.

Possible Uses
Flowers.
Snow flakes (used individually).
Any lumpy area.

8. Stem Stitch

Worked in rows moving DOWN instead of left to right. For first row, start with a tent stitch, increasing to four vertical and four horizontal and keeping that count all the way down for first stripe decreasing at end down to tent stitch.

Second row or stripe: Turn canvas sideways, and start at bottom of first row, increase from tent stitch out to four vertical and four horizontal and work to right until you decrease at end of row down to tent stitch.

Caution: If you don't end up with a tent stitch (a stitch covering one intersection of canvas), you've missed a hole some place or gone into the same hole twice. Pull yarn out and do over if that is the case.

For Wallhanging
Use two-ply. Large rectangle.

Possible Uses
Fences
Use wherever vertical stripe is needed.

9. Star or Algerian Eye

Always go to back or down at center of star so you don't cut your yarn. Keep a tight tension and work your way around square leaving a nice hole in center. (Center would be even numbered if shown.) Each star is over four vertical and four horizontal threads.

Caution: If your tension isn't tight, the threads of yarn will overlap and you will not have a center hole.

For Wallhanging
Use three-ply. Small rectangle.
First color.

Possible Uses
Frame or border.
As a flower.

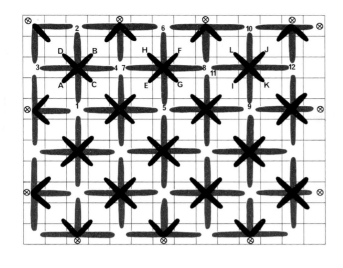

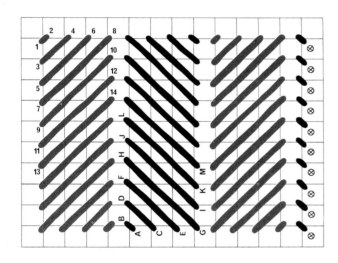

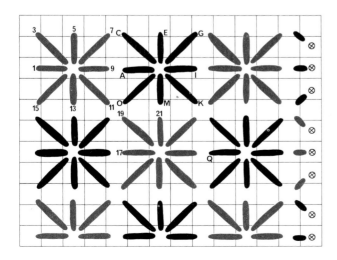

10. Mosaic or Diagonal Hungarian

Done on the diagonal for two colors, the stitch is done with a tent, slanted gobelin, and tent to form a small square. Between six and seven straighten needle vertically and go under two horizontal threads. At end of row, hold first color and starting at top left again do second row in second color, then turn upside down and return with first color. Notice long stitches touch long stitches of same color.

For Wallhanging
Two-ply. Same colors as other large rectangles.

Possible Uses
Excellent to use as background of sampler or motto where words are done in tent stitch became it compensates perfectly around them (the words) as the name implies, it looks like a mosaic tile.

11. Rice Stitch

Composite stitch: Worked in rows from left to right over count of four horizontal and four vertical. Starting at bottom left, scoop between two and three, four and five, six and seven, etc.
Top: Covering arms of the bottom cross stitch at all four corners, when you finish you will have a design of diamond shapes.

For Wallhanging
Use three-ply on bottom and two ply on top.
Small rectangle.

Possible Uses
Frame or border.

12. Diamond Eyelet

Come up at one. Using quite a strong tension, go down in center coming up at three. You might notice that three is over one thread and up one thread of canvas from one. Follow this procedure to nine and turn your canvas one-quarter turn to seventeen. Turn one-quarter and proceed the same way to twenty-five when you'll turn one-quarter again to thirty-one. Always go down at the center of your diamond so you don't cut the thread.

For Wallhanging
Use two-ply. Large rectangle.

Possible Uses
Stylized pineapple.
Jester's jacket.

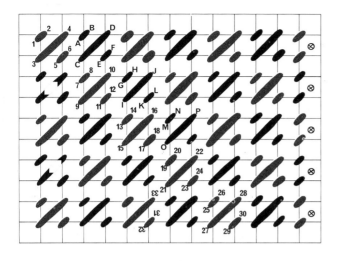

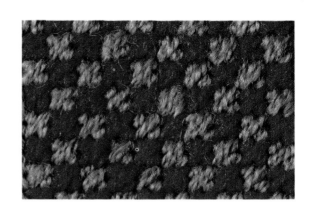

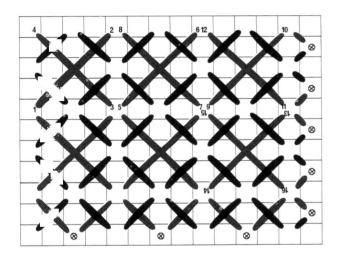

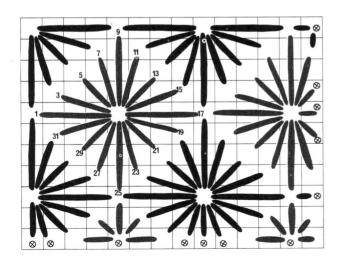

13. Monogram and Continental Tent

CONTINENTAL TENT: This is the only stitch which must be started from right to left. The needle is kept slanted and after coming out at one, is scooped from two to three, four to five, etc. At the end of the row take needle to back of canvas, turn upside down, and return using same count. When you reach a tent stitch already filled in with your initials, just skip over it and continue the row.

For Wallhanging
Use three-ply.
See page 84 for monograms.
Using a piece of graph paper and a pencil, pick out your three initials on the alphabet shown. First, you must remember that your small rectangle is over 12 horizontal and 56 vertical threads of canvas. You will see that the alphabet used is over 8 horizontal threads or eight tent stitches up and down. There will be two horizontal threads left empty at bottom and top of rectangle which will be filled with background (Continental Tent) later. Count the number of squares in each letter of your own monogram from the alphabet

going from left to right. Allow at least one vertical thread to separate each letter of your monogram which brings my particular monogram up to twenty-seven. Divide by two for the space left on each side of the monogram. Following the graph you have worked out from page 84, put in your monogram in the deepest shade and color you have chosen. (You may also wish to put in a little design to fill in the space as I did.) Start your tent stitches as you write from bottom to top and left to right. Fill in the background with Continental Tent Stitch in the lightest shade you have.

15. Buttonhole or Blanket

Coming out at one below third horizontal thread of canvas, drop yarn down toward lap. Holding yarn down with left thumb, scoop between two and three. Drop yarn down each time and hold tension with the left thumb so all little ridges at bottom are even. Note: When ending one piece of yarn, go to back at bottom right. When starting again, start at ridge already made. This means one ridge will be over the other that one time so keep tight tension. This stitch may not be turned upside down as ridges would meet. It may be done from right to left but ridges will be reversed. Depends on look desired.

For Wallhanging
Small rectangle, use different color for each row. Three-ply.

16. Hungarian Ground

All straight Gobelin stitches worked first row over four horizontal threads moving up and down the row in series of three.
Second row: in another color over two horizontal threads in series of four stitches forming diamond shape.
Third row: Same as first using first color but comes up and meets first row on third stitch.

Note: This is rumoured to be the forerunner of Flame Stitch.

For Wallhanging
Use three-ply. Large rectangle.

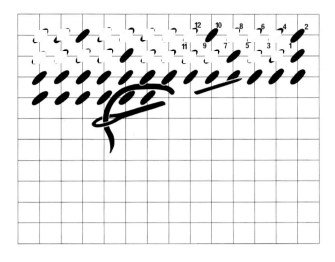

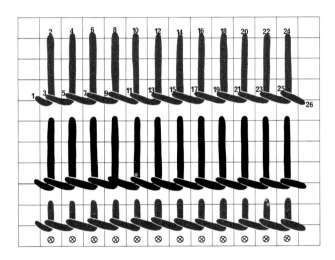

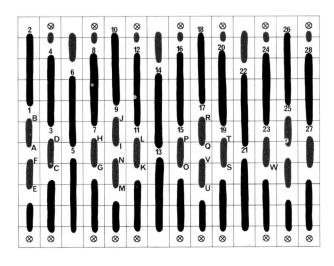

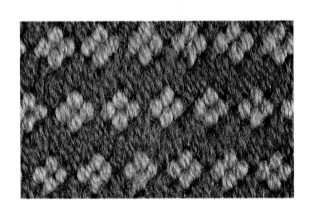

17. Reverse Tent Stitch

First row: Turning canvas sideways so top is to right, come up at one scooping from two to three, four to five, etc.
Second row: This row is really Continental Tent started from right to left. Come up at one, scoop from two to three etc.
Third row: Same as first.
Fourth row: Same as second.

For Wallhanging
Use three-ply. Small rectangle.

Possible Uses
When a knitted look is desired use this stitch.

18. Brick Stitch

Worked straight sideways over four vertical threads zigzagging each stitch down the canvas.
Up from back at one, scoop from two to three, four to five etc.

For Wallhanging
Use three-ply. Large rectangle.

Possible Uses
This stitch usually done in only one color to look like real bricks and works beautifully for a fast background.
Sides on houses.
Tiles of roof.
Stylized shading.

19. Leaf Stitch

First stitch over two horizontal threads. Second over two horizontal and one vertical thread, third, fourth, and fifth over two horizontal and two vertical. Leaves in rows fitting into each other. Second color, first stitch over two horizontal and two vertical, second stitch over two horizontal, third stitch over two horizontal and two vertical.

For Wallhanging
Three-ply in needle. Use a different color for each row. Small rectangle.

Possible Uses
As feathers on birds, wings on chickens etc.
Leaves on trees.

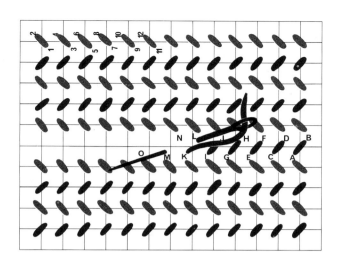

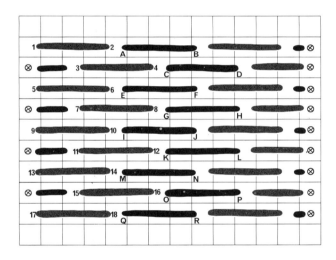

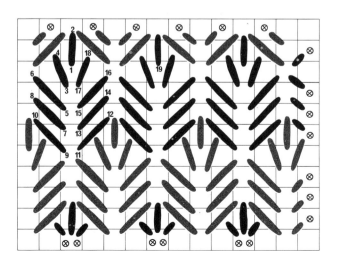

20. Moorish Stitch

First stitch is really a tent stitch going from bottom left to top right crossing one intersection of canvas. Second, third, and fourth stitches are slanted gobelin stitches going over two horizontal and two vertical, three horizontal and three vertical, and two horizontal and two vertical, respectively back to a tent stitch moving diagonally down the canvas. Between each row start at bottom of area making tent stitches and work up.

For Wallhanging
Two-ply first color, three-ply second color (tent). Large rectangle.

Possible Uses
Roof tops.
Stairs
Geometric designs worked four ways out from center.

21. Long Legged Cross

One-ply when over two horizontal threads and two-ply when over four horizontal threads of canvas. This stitch has two secrets; after coming up at one, keep needle vertical at all times. Then after making a simple cross stitch (2 to 3, 4 to 5,) learn a simple rule. "Forward 3 and back 2." You will see that from five to six is FORWARD 3 vertical threads or into the empty space. From 7 to 8 is BACK 2 vertical threads. Once you have the rhythm it is easy.

For Wallhanging
First and fourth rows over 2 horizontal from left to right.
Second and third rows over 4 horizontal from left to right.
Small rectangle.

Possible Uses
This stitch is ideal for finishing pillows, wall hangings, trivets, purses, coasters, etc. May be worked over any number of horizontal threads but keeps same count vertically.

22. Milanese

Composed of slanted Gobelin stitches the secret here is to watch your needle when scooping from eight to nine. Nine should be over two vertical and up one from number seven. Always say to yourself, "over two and up one." When you start second row you should turn upside down and start smallest stitch along same angle (in same hole) as longest stitch from first row. If you are unsure of compensation, in area to be filled do several rows and then you can see around the edge of area how the stitches should be.

For Wallhanging
Use two-ply in large rectangle.

Possible Uses
Gives 3 D effect when used coming out in V shape.

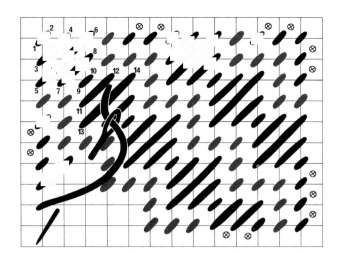

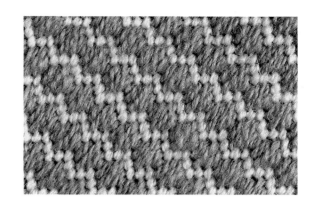

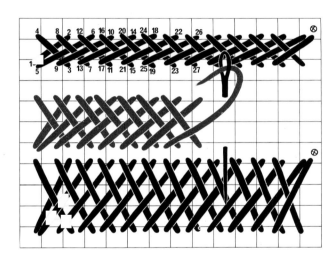

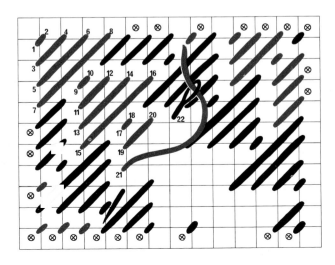

23. Straight Cross

Worked over two horizontal and two vertical threads bottom to top and left to right.

Second row fits into first row between stitches usually in another color.

For Wallhanging
Two-ply. Small rectangle.
Top and bottom compensation do not necessarily end up in same color.

Possible Uses
This stitch is good for flower centers.

25. Backstitch

Come up from back of canvas two threads down at number one. Scoop under four threads between two and three, four and five, etc.

Note: If you don't want backstitch to be noticeable use same color as stitch (that you are going around.) Use another color if accent is desired.

Although color picture is Star or Algerian Eyelet Stitch (you will have noticed), I have used another stitch (Backstitch) between the Star Stitches. This is to cover exposed canvas. Sometimes used between rows of stitches (such as Oblong Cross Stitch) or between the stitches themsedves)as with Diamond Eyelet). Usually one ply of yarn is sufficient to cover canvas if loose tension is used and usually you will turn the canvas sideways to start.

For Wallhanging
Use between rows of Oblong Cross Stitch with one-ply of yarn if canvas shows. Use alternate color and light tension. Turn canvas sideways to work between rows. Also, use backstitch around diamond eyelet and use two stitches per side of diamond. Use around Star stitch too if needed with two stitches per side.
In crewel it may be used for stems on flowers or wherever an outline is needed.

26. Jacquard

Using slanted Gobelin Stitches, start with two compensation stitches. The real stitches start with number five on the diagram. It is over three vertical and three horizontal threads of canvas.
FOR THE FIRST TIME, COUNT STITCHES, NOT NUMBERS.
Count this way: 1, 2, 3, 4, 5, and 5 is 1, 2, 3, 4, 5, and 5, is 1. You will see that it is five stitches over and

five stitches down, then five stitches over etc. in steps like stairs. The trick here is to remember that the fifth stitch over is also the same one as the first stitch down. After doing several "steps", stop and count to see if you are right. The rows on either side are tent stitch.
Note: Byzantine Stitch is worked the same way leaving out rows of tent stitch.

For Wallhanging
Two-ply. Large rectangle alternate for Moorish stitch.

Possible Uses
Same as Moorish Stitch # 20.

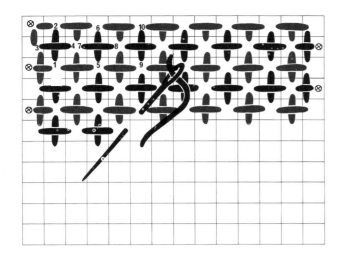

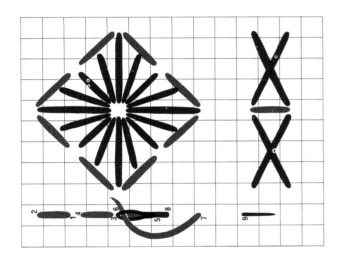

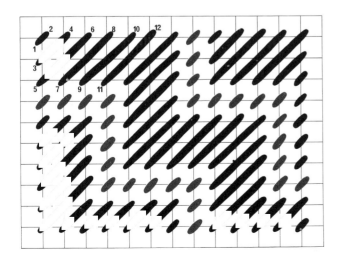

27. Raised Spider or Rosebud

In center of Diagonal Tent rectangle, make a five-point star always going down at center. Bring needle up as close to center (but not in center) as possible at eleven. Weave needle over and under spokes of star pulling yarn towards center until all spokes are covered. Take needle to back of canvas, weave through, and cut off excess yarn.

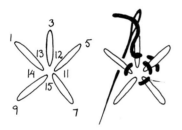

28. Couching (Steam of Flower)

Come up at one and hold yarn to make a curved stem going down at two. Still holding yarn, couch down with two or three small stitches to hold the curve.

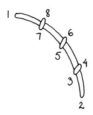

29. Detached Chain (long part of leaves)

Step One: Coming up at one, catch yarn under three as you scoop from two to three.

Step Two: Pull yarn through three until it looks like a leaf and latch it or couch it down at four with a small stitch.

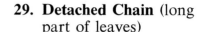

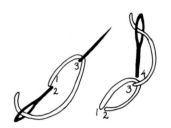

30. Fly Stitch (Drooping part of leaf)

Come up at one, drop yarn down and scoop from two to three catching yarn and go down at four to finish stitch. This is really an open chain stitch.

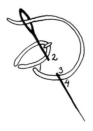

31. Chain Stitch (Optional to decorate with instead of flower making own design)

One, drop yarn down, put needle back in same hole and scoop from two to three catching yarn under needle making loop. Again put needle into three and scoop to four catching yarn. Always go down in center of loop. This is not a long wearing stitch on canvas unless used over another stitch like diagonal tent.

32. French Knot (Optional to use in center of Diamond or Algerian Eyelet)

Come up at one, with left hand wrap yarn once around needle and go down at one again keeping tight tension on yarn with left hand. To be done correctly, you should have a dimple in center of knot. Normally you only wrap needle once but if used in center of eyelet it is better to wrap twice so it doesn't pull through or use more yarn in needle.

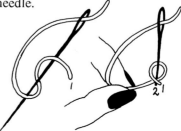

Usually when it comes to shading in a piece of canvas work or crewel we have a choice of from three to five colors of yarn. If your design calls for five shades of one color and you can only buy three shades you can make the second and fourth shades by separating the yarns and putting the first and third shade together to make the second, and the third and fifth to make the fourth. See first drawing.

Sometimes you hear blending or shading of yarns called needle painting. This is an apt name for it because it takes some skill to know when to change the shade of hue (color) in your needle. If it (the canvas) has been painted by someone who really knows needlepoint, the changes will be very apparent, but if they are blended so you cannot really tell, it is up to you to decide when to change shades of color in your needle. With crewel it is a little more complicated as only the outline of the major design is there and you are following a picture beside you. The easiest way to decide where the light should fall is to imagine a window to your upper left. Where the light first hits is the lightest, around the middle of the design is medium light, and at the bottom right is the darkest. See second drawing.

You can also imagine the light coming from behind you and then the center of the design would be the lightest and shading off on either side to the darkest. See third drawing.

Shading

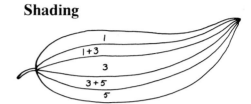

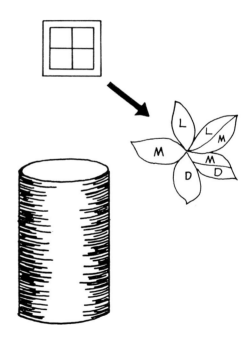

MOST NEEDLEPOINT STITCHES MAY BE USED IN CREWEL WORK
MOST CREWEL STITCHES MAY BE USED ON CANVAS

24. Swedish Rya, Turkey Tufting or Ghiordes Knot

Keep needle horizontal at all times. Worked from left to right going under one vertical thread at a time. STARTED FROM FRONT OF CANVAS AND FROM BOTTOM OF AREA TO BE FILLED.

After taking first step from one to two, throw yarn up and scoop from three to four. Throw yarn down catching yarn with left thumb to make a loop. Scoop from five to six. Throw yarn up and repeat.

Once yarn is pulled tight at four, may be cut at any time to change color, etc. Each stitch is locked. If same color is used (as is true on the wallhanging), wait until you use up all yarn in needle and then cut loops. Always worked from left to right, and never turned upside down.

Note: Learn rhythm by saying to yourself "Throw it up, throw it down". Fringe can be left in loops if you are careful to make loops even. Never cut loops less than 3/4

of an inch short as knots will come untied. Length of pile depends on how large loop is.

For Wallhanging

Use two-ply bottom and top. Fringe at bottom, use three-ply, filling up remaining space of bottom rectangle.

Possible Uses

Excellent for rugs, fur on animals, fringe, etc.

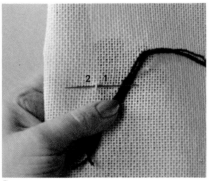
Step one

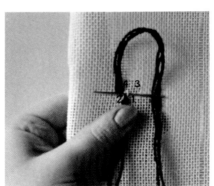
Step two

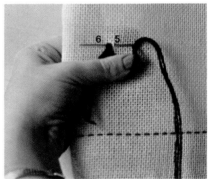
Step three

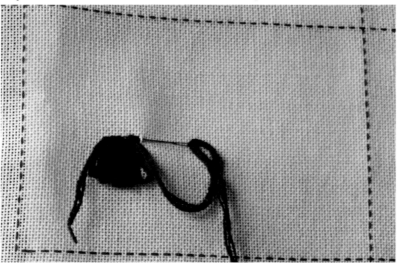

Swedish Rya: Be sure you use a yarn that will fluff out well when cut and DON'T cut loops too short or rows of stitches will show.

Small Bear

Wrong—cut too short

Big Bear

Right

14. Diagonal Tent Stitch

This stitch is the most longwearing and versatile stitch there is. It does not get the canvas out of shape as does Continental Tent. You never turn the canvas for this stitch. Looking at the canvas you will see that the squares of thread meet at intersections that weave in and out with a vertical thread on top at one intersection and a horizontal thread on top at the next intersection. This is important to remember to work this stitch on mono canvas.

1. Worked by going down the ladder covering vertical intersections of canvas from bottom left of intersection to top right with the needle always vertical scooping under two horizontal threads between stitches.

2. To come back up the ladder the needle is horizontal and covers the horizontal intersection of canvas from bottom left to top right scooping under two vertical threads of canvas between stitches.

This stitch forms a basketweave on the back of the canvas. The rows move from right to left as completed.

For Wallhanging
Do triangle in one color, the right hand triangle in same color, and fill in with second color. Third color is used for floral decoration.

1. Going down

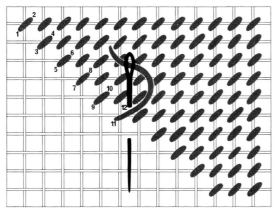

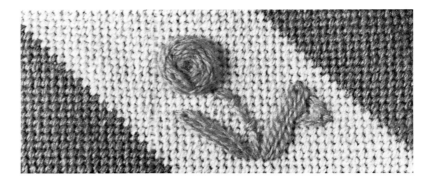

2. Going up

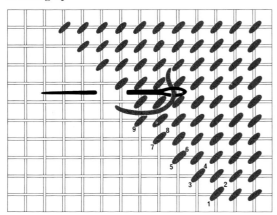

Assuming you have already bought your Woolite, nails, hammer and board for blocking, we can go on to washing, blocking, and finishing your wallhanging.

Remove tape and hem sides on sewing machine or by hand. This is to keep your bellpull from raveling the unworked canvas during washing. Wash in Woolite in cold water, rinse, and roll up in large towel squeezing gently to remove excess water. While washing do not scrub or wring out.

Never put nails through your finished needlepoint. That is why we have left unworked canvas so we can nail in this area. Block by nailing into the unworked canvas onto a board. Be sure it is FACE UP so that the stitches aren't crushed while they dry. You must keep a strong tension and put nails across from each other each time until you have no scalloping left. Let dry for two days, away from pets and preferably flat. Be sure your sides are even all the way around when blocking, by lining off board both horizontally and vertically by the inch. See blocking pictures page 101.

Finishing Bellpull or Wallhanging

Washing and Blocking

Blocking

65

Finishing for Wallhanging

After cutting your velveteen down to fit the bellpull plus 1/2 inch for hem on all four sides, cut off excess unworked canvas on sides leaving five unworked vertical threads to turn back. Do not cut top or bottom selvage off. Baste a thread along both sides on front so you have exact line to follow when turned over. (This is because some stitches don't have an exact line to follow on back.) Put right side of velveteen and right side of needlepoint together and baste. Sew ice cream sticks at top and bottom of bellpull horizontally on back side of worked canvas to keep it straight when hung.

Sew three drapery weights in a row at bottom of worked canvas on back side to hold bellpull down when hung.

On sewing machine or by hand start sewing from bottom to top on the long side. Do second long side from bottom to top so that if there is any give both sides will give in same direction. Finish both top and bottom by hand after first turning right sides out and tucking in hems. Remove basting threads.

Take one drapery ring and same color yarn as used for fringe. Holding ring and two inches of yarn in left hand (after first threading three-ply yarn on tapestry needle), do the same buttonhole stitch used on sampler except slipping the needle through the hole of the ring instead of the canvas. Keep going around ring until ring is solidly covered. Still keeping tight tension, sew ring onto bellpull at top between 14th and 15th oblong cross-stitch, slip needle off remaining yarn and tie two or three knots with leftover beginning and ending yarn, and your bellpull is finished and ready to hang on the wall.

Diaper Patterns over Four Threads

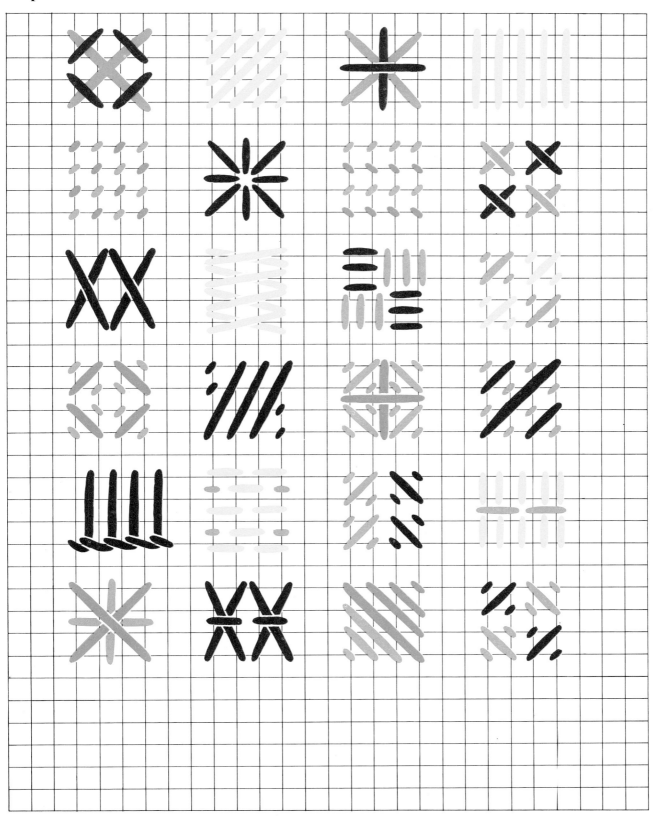

Diaper Patterns over Six Threads

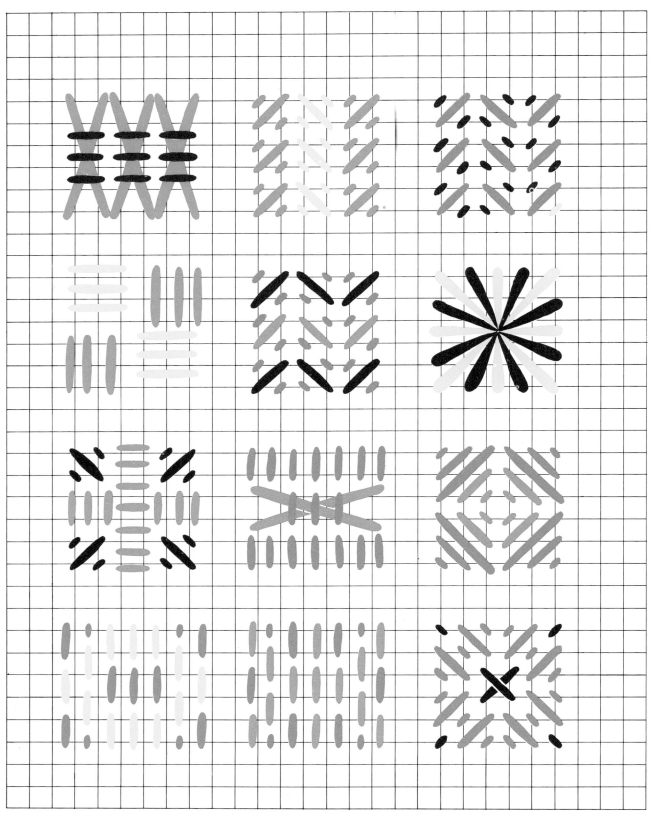

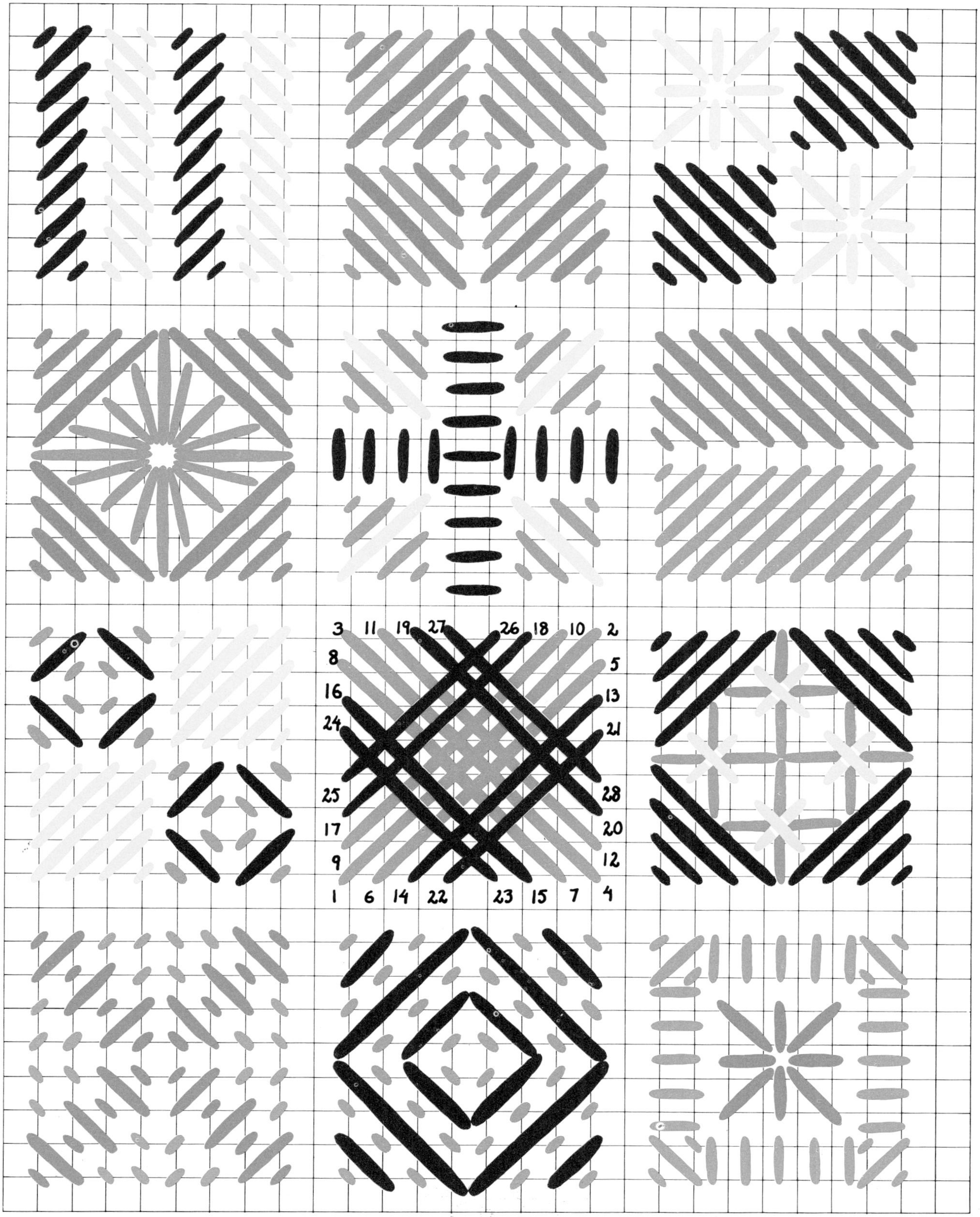
3 11 19 27 26 18 10 2
8
16
24
25
17
9
5
13
21
28
20
12
1 6 14 22 23 15 7 4

The complementary color scheme is striking when one color is used full chroma (the red), and the other color in softer shades (the green).

The Conspiracy Seven

What are these bogeymen, the big Seven? Are they the Mafia that no one speaks about openly? Of course not, they are simply the rules you must follow in order to make a good design. Now, if anyone brings up modern art where the Seven are concerned, I admit these rules break down sometimes. But famous artists know how and when to break the rules; I'm not putting you or myself in their class. They have spent a lifetime developing the talent and skills they possess. Most of us are not in that category. If you are an artist, I can only help you in the techniques used to paint this type of canvas. What I'm really trying to do is help the nonprofessional who likes to do things with her hands, has the leisure time to do it, and wants to learn the basics.

Here are the magic Seven and I hope that after designing a piece of needlework and before putting your design on canvas or material, you will stop and check to see if you have carried through on all of the Seven before proceeding.

Proportion

This is the satisfactory relationship in scale between all the varied units composing a design, and between the design itself and its adjoining areas of undecorated ground fabric, whether canvas or material.

Focal Point

This means the emphasizing of a certain part of the design and understressing of others to just the right degree. The physical eye needs this stimulus when viewing any work of decorative art such as needlepoint. The first visual impact is made at the Focal Point. Lacking a focal point, a design will tend to become a monotonous rambling pattern of shapes without meaning. A focal point in embroidery can be achieved by using a different thickness of thread, or by introducing a contrasting color, texture, variation in scale, change in stitch, or by any of these combinations.

Repetition or Rhythm

The ear responds to the beat of the drum in music, and the eye responds in the same manner to color, stitch, and shape in needlepoint and crewel. This implies repetition so do not introduce a color note only in one spot. Such a spot will stop your eye abruptly. A pleasing sequence in scale and proportion influences the rhythm in your design. Each shape should be in harmony with the other shapes. Thus, circles, egg shapes, ovals, kidney shapes are in harmony, but if you added a square it would not be harmonious. Also, you should never have a fifty-fifty distribution of color.

Contrast

A well-ordered change from a stright line to a curve, from a rough to a smooth texture, from thick to thin yarn, from light to dark colors, and from medium to big or small shapes can make our designs more exciting. Contrasting colors and values appear quite differently when seen side by side than when segregated and seen apart. The colors seem brighter, and lighter values more luminous in contrast, while darker appears even darker.

Balance

In most of us, balance is an instinct. In good design, optical balance as well as physical balance is required. Warm colors have more visual weight than cool ones, brilliant colors more than greyed ones. Light colors have less visual weight then dark colors. If all intense or dark color is concentrated on one side of a design without compensating weight on the other, the composition will seem to tip over on the dark side.

Symmetrical Balance

A design then, is like an old fashioned scale with a center balance pin with both sides of the same weight or force, and if there is to be perfect balance.

Areas in a composition are positive and negative; the things and the spaces left around them. These must be arranged so that the whole holds together as a unit. It is better not to place a strong interest at the center or central axis, either vertically or horizontally (see Golden Mean). Elements whose axis or contours are parallel to the sides of the composition are more static than those which are not so related to the frame. By pointing shapes directly out to the corner, the eye may be led away from the main interest. It is better not to create shapes which are tangent to themselves or to the edges of the composition unless you intend to create a feeling of tension.

If an object is nearer the edge of the composition than it is to other objects within the embroidery, the design lacks unity. The area between objects in the embroidery should be less than the area which surrounds the objects.

Asymmetrical Balance

Asymmetrical Balance is the other type of balance. The objects are balanced by their placement on the canvas. This is harder to achieve than symmetrical balance. The stronger colors, textures, etc., should be towards the imaginary center axis and the light ones towards the outer edges. It also means the felt equality between the parts of the field by controlling the opposing attractions. It does not have a central point of explicit axis. A psychological center of gravity must be present, however. The absence of actual axis or focal center emphasizes the relativity of all the elements of the field. Secondly, it means opposing elements that are different rather than alike. You can balance a small area of strong color in one part of the field by a large area of empty space in another. In art, it is a matter of secure, mature, sensitive judgement in the use of the varying parts involved.

Color

Color is so important, I have given it a special section under CAPTIVATING COLOR, page 88.

Unity

The final aim of any design should be unity, that certain quality of completeness brought about through the cooperation of every aspect of a decorative idea ... design, color, material, method and function. There are certain artistic rules which must be observed if this is to be achieved. Our laws of design are derived from those in nature, and though we may do so unconsciously, we use nature as our ideal standard for judging art.

Design might be accurately described as an ordered arrangement of separate forms controlled by geometric equations. But you cannot design just by geometry. We do put shapes into certain mathematical relationships but we must also be aware of our own eye for the appropriate shape, and how we space these forms and allow our own good taste to show through. The success or failure of a piece of needlepoint or crewel must rest on the individual's knowledge of the fundamentals or principles of design and the manner in which she "reaches out" to achieve it in the most pleasing and creative way.

When the design you may have found comes out of a magazine and happens to be two inches by two inches, and you want to use it for a pillow that is fourteen by fourteen, what do you do to make the design in the size you want?

There is a formula that is a little tricky but workable if you remember a few simple rules. However, before I give you this information, let me say that you can forget the formula and cheat a little by taking the design to the nearest photocopier and have it done for you to your dimensions. You should get the man to give you the positive which has black lines on white paper. It's not expensive and saves a lot of time.

If you're camped out in the Rockies and you only have my book and a ruler, here's how to go about it.

First off, remember that you have to enlarge it IN PROPORTION to the smaller version. (I forgot to do this the first time I enlarged anything and had the longest guitar anybody ever saw.) In other words, if it is one inch by one inch, you must enlarge the square to two inches by two inches, not two and three-fourths by one and a-half inches.

You must line off the small piece you want to copy in squares. Then, in proportion to the small piece, you line off the piece you want to do in the proper size. Anythink that is in the first little square you put in the first big square and so on until the whole picture has been transferred.

If it is too large, and you wish to make it smaller, it follows that you will just reverse the process.

If it gets too hectic for you, or you are like me and hate anything mathmatical, play dumb, and let your big bright husband or boy friend do that part for you. It will get him in the act, make him feel important, and you can be making him a drink in the meantime to keep in his good graces. (I call it playing "Magnolia" as the southern belles did in the old days.) Just say to him, "Sweetheart, I know you're so good at mechanical things, and I never could understand geometry, so would you mind looking at this and explaining it to me?" Maybe you should make the drink first, to get him in the right receptive mood. By the time he's explained it, it should be practically finished. Good luck, you "Magnolias" out there.

To Increase or Decrease, That is The Question

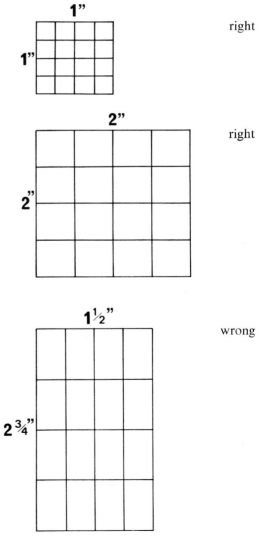

You may also increase or decrease a design or picture by taking the design to a photocopier and have him enlarge it. Ask for the positive.

Joining Canvas. Remove seven threads from each side and weave together. Be sure both sides are same size mesh.

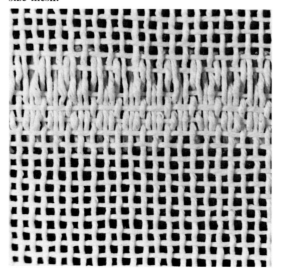

Repaired Hole. Cut square in same size mesh, twice as large as hole. Remove five threads and weave in and out on all four sides.

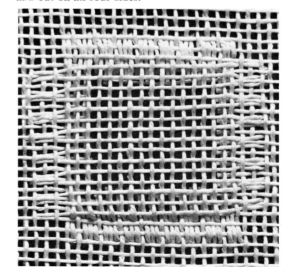

When deciding on a design, it sometimes take the shape of a hobby. If you like horses, dogs, trains, cars, or whatever, it is a good idea to take your hobby or that of anyone you wish to make a piece for, and depict it in needlepoint or crewel.

If it is horseback riding, for instance, it is better to use three horses than two. Why? If something is balanced evenly, (that is, two, four, or six) it tends to be monotonous. If it is asymmetrical, it is more pleasing to the eye and holds more interest and, if it is placed in a triangle, keeps your eye within the picture.

Look around you right now at the drapes, upholstery fabric, or wallpaper. Count the numbers and I bet it will be three or five. Just for fun in the next few days, look at every print you see whether it is on the blouse of the lady next door, the design in the magazine you read, or the advertisement you receive through the mail. I'll make a bet with you that most of the designs you will see will follow this rule. I think it is one of the most important pieces of information you can have on design.

Look at the skiers on page fifteen, and see the Theory of Three in action. She has used many triangles and five (or seven) major shapes. Try using this theory the next time you compose a design.

Don't Be a Square

Theory of Three

If many colors and shades are used, separate and unify by surrounding them with one color and stitch.

Stick to three colors or shades when stitches are put side by side using one dark, one light, one bright.

Eyeglasses and checkbooks may be finished yourself with long-legged cross to bind it together.

Belts are a good way to practice stitches and still make something inexpensive.

Children love animals and here is where many stitches may be used to advantage.

Sculpted Swedish Rya gives a 3-D or padded look.

Lettering is the only time that you must work the words or letters out on graph paper first.

Remember to count the spaces between letters too. Leave at least one space between letters and two spaces between words.

Golden Mean

Another rule that helps is the Golden Mean. If you are a mathematician, an architect, or an engineer, this will immediately ring a bell. If you are not, it sounds like something to do with Greek mythology. At least, it did to me when I first heard it. It is something the Greeks really did discover and everyone has been using since. It is what makes most of our books in the shape they are, the paper we write on the rectangle it is, and many more.

It means that they discovered that the most pleasing rectangle is one in which you take a square (any size square), put one-half of that square on the side of the whole square, and the rectangle formed is the perfect rectangle. The line that separates the square from the half square is the GOLDEN MEAN.

There is a geometric equation for this. It is in Graves' "The Art of Color and Design," which is an excellent reference book on design. My mind just doesn't work that way. Besides, my method is simpler and it works.

Why do I give you the GOLDEN MEAN? What use can you put it to? The reason is: it is better to place your focal point along The GOLDEN MEAN than centered. The GOLDEN MEAN emphasizes this point which is so important.

If you are lining up a group of buildings along a street for example, it would be better to place your largest, most impressive building on the GOLDEN MEAN.

Rearranging or taking part of an existing design or putting forms from different designs together must be done with taste and forethought. These two rules will be of help. Consider them your best friends.

Proverbs and Patience

Needlepoint and crewel books are filled with black-and-white graphs for design. These are good if you have lots of patience and want an exact replica of someone else's work. I feel that in designing or translating an existing design it is much easier to paint in the design. Then you have some leeway to move to the left or right, up or down, without adjusting the whole graph.

The only time it is not only preferable but mandatory to use a graph is when lettering or numbers come into your design. Sometimes you will want a graph too if it is strictly a geometric and then you only have to do 1/4 of the design on graph paper and turn it around. See page 21.

With lettering you must know certain things. How many threads of the canvas does the alphabet I am using go over horizontally? I am including a five (the smallest) and two eight horizontal-thread alphabets, as I think they are the most useful for putting in your initials or name on pillows, etc.

As an example, let's pretend you have to get three initials spaced evenly between twenty-five vertical and twelve horizontal threads. Using the eight horizontal alphabet, if for example, your initials are B.H.D. you will see that each initial is over six vertical threads. You must have at least one space between your letters. Because it is an eight horizontal alphabet, we know that we will have two blanks at the top and two at the bottom to make twelve. Adding the six, six, and six vertical we have eighteen. Then to put a space between the three letters we add two more to make twenty. When you come out with an odd number to divide for the spacing at beginning and end, as will happen if you have five spaces left, put two at the beginning and the three at the end. Your eye is more used to seeing larger gaps at the end.

In other words, it would look like the following graph.

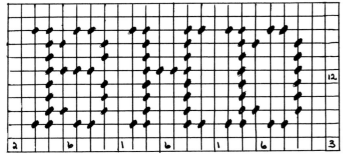

If you do a man's vest, for a further example, you would use the more masculine alphabet with block letters to personalize it. If it is to be a feminine pillow for a girl's bedroom, the script would be more in keeping.

The smallest alphabet that seems to be successful is one over five horizontal threads. Anything smaller and the letters tend to look like one another.

Do not feel that you have to use the alphabets exactly as they are. If you do not like a particular letter, change it a little to your liking. Also, if you have letters that go off to the left like a, m, n, r, v, w or x, feel free to turn the tent stitch to the left instead of the right. I don't know how legitimate it may be but it certainly looks better. Experiment a bit and don't feel badly if you have to pull some of it out. We all have to do it sooner or later. It's not that hard to do. Just be sure to pick it out with a needle and don't let a scissors near the canvas. A cut canvas can be hard to fix.

When making up your own lettering for a saying, proverb, or axiom, get large graph paper, do each word, cut the words out, and place over another paper until the whole thing looks balanced. If you have miscalculated somehow and find you have space left, you can always do a pretty little design at the end.

For Crewel Lettering

With crewel, you can be just as simple or just as fancy as you please. You can work your initials into the design, spell out your whole name in script, or embellish it with flowers. The choice is practically unlimited.

Some of the favorite stitches to use are chain, stem, backstitch, or split stitch. My own preference is chain as you can weave another color yarn through it for a charming effect. Don't forget cross-stitch too!

There is a marvelous little series of books put out by Dollfus-Mieg and Cie, better known as DMC, which has numerous alphabets in cross-stitch that are graphed out so you can adapt for needlepoint or crewel. They are inexpensive and they come five booklets to the set.

For larger alphabets, I like a booklet by Doris Drake called **Needlework Designs,** Thomasville, Georgia 31792.

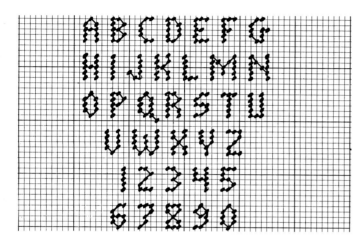

The five horizontal alphabet is the smallest I could devise, and may be used for whole words or initials. The eight horizontal alphabets are good to use just for initials. I like to see your needlepoint and crewel dated as it means so much to future generations to know when it was made. Don't be afraid to make up your own initials in any size you prefer. Buy graph paper to work them out.

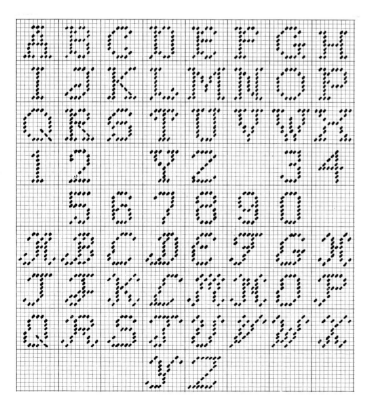

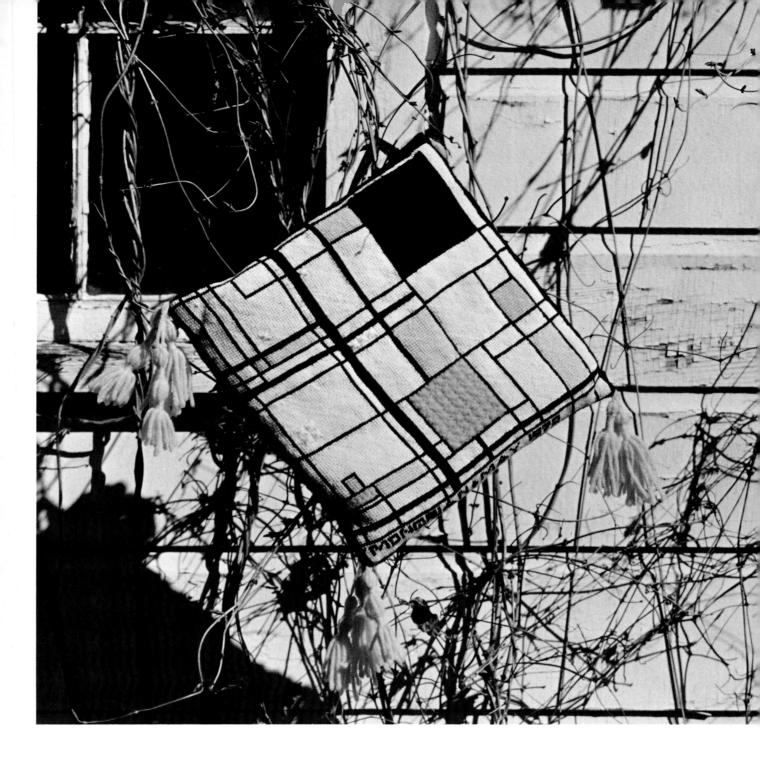

This adaptation of Mondrian could well be
a focal point for your whole room.

87

Captivating Color

How Color Affects You

Color is such a personal th_ng. Each color has some special meaning or memory connected with it which determines whether or not we like it. Sometimes we like to wear a color but would not think of using it in the color scheme of our home, or vice versa. One of the things we should keep in mind when trying to decide on a color scheme for a particular design is where the piece is going to be placed when finished.

If a pillow, for example, has been designed from the print of a chair that is in your living room, and it is going to be placed on a plain couch, the color scheme has already been established. On the other hand, if it is a gift for a new bride and you know she loves blue and is very modern, it is a wee bit more complicated. You must determine as subtly as possible what her accent colors are going to be or use many shades of blue and perhaps a white. Then you have to find a design possibly in an abstract that can use those shades of color in a flattering way.

If you have no idea what colors are in a friend's home and yet you want to give her a gift of needlepoint or crewel, it is a better idea to make something personal that she can use, such as an eyeglass case, belt, or a purse, and which she can coordinate easily.

I would suggest to anyone who is doing their own designing, to first buy a color wheel in any paint shop, and then make a yarn wheel to give ideas of colors and shades of yarns available in her area.

The Color Schemes

Everyone, I assume, knows that the **primary colors** are yellow, blue, and red. They also know that the **secondary colors** are mixtures of the primaries. Thus, red and yellow make orange, blue and red make violet and blue and yellow make green. **Intermediate colors** are obtained by mixing adjoining primary+secondary colors. **Tertiary colors** are mixed from secondary colors:
Turquoise from green and blue
Purple from violet and red
Scarlet from red and orange

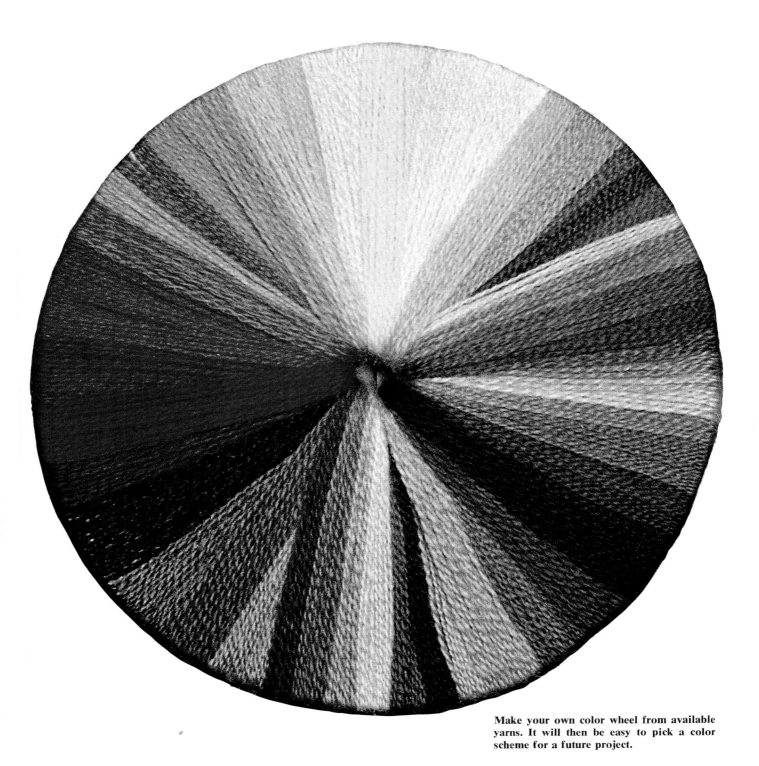

Make your own color wheel from available yarns. It will then be easy to pick a color scheme for a future project.

Complementary

Complementary Color Schemes are easy to use, such as red and green, or blue and orange. They are directly across from one another on the color wheel. I hope you have made. It is more pleasing to the eye if you use one of them in softened shades (values), or separate them by using either black or white in between.

Analogous

An **Analogous Color Scheme** is always pretty. This consists of one primary and the colors alongside it. There is a difference of opinion as to whether you can say it consists of one primary and two secondary colors or more. In any case don't introduce too many colors or shades into your design or it will lack unity. An example of an analogous scheme would be yellow, orange, and green (as seen on page 41 on the second bellpull from the left).

Monochromatic

A **Monochromatic Color Scheme** can be very dramatic and a challenge in finding just the right shades of yarn to complement your design. This is made up of shades of one color and perhaps a black or white added.

Hue

Hue is just another name for color. When you add white to a basic color, you develop a **tint.** When you add black to a color, you get a **shade.** When mixing your colors, remember that when you make a tint it is better to start with the white and add the hue (color). When you make a shade, it is better to start with the hue and add black. A color made from mixing colors is never as bright as the original or primary color. If you have too bright a color in a design, use a contrasting color to dull it down a bit.

Although you can keep adding colors, if you get too many together the mixture just becomes a dirty grey. Colors may be dulled down or brightened up depending on what colors or hues are used alongside them. Black next to a color makes it look brighter.

Value

Value could be called another name for the different shades of hue. On a scale of one to ten, if you were going from black to white, one would be black, and ten would be white.

Chroma

Chroma is the purity, intensity, or strength of a color. Therefore, colors are more contrasting when their chromas are strong, and get along better together when their chromas are softer.

Cocktail napkins are simple sources of design which work up excitingly in stitchery. Textured stitches are all important here.

Vests showing your man's hobbies will be a favorite with him.

When mixing colors, it is better to start out blending your colors softly and subtly.

Something else to be noted about the color of yarns: usually the lighter the yarn, the more strands you will need to cover the canvas. This is because the darker the dye the more it "draws up" or thickens the yarn. Sometimes the uniformity depends on the expertness of the weaver or the way the fibers are woven, and you will get variations in thickness due to the weather when the yarn was woven.

GET ALL YOUR BACKGROUND COLOR at one time and compare each skein to see that it is all from the same dye lot. Take it to the window for natural light. Never depend on artificial light to pick your colors.

A word to the wise: There has been a good deal of unhappiness due to the person not buying enough yarn and not being able to match it later. Most good embroidery shops will let you return any unused ounces as long as it has been kept untangled and **clean** so it may be resold. So, please BUY ENOUGH OR MORE.

The difference in yarns can also affect how the color looks. A rayon, silk or cotton will be shinier and brighter than wool yarns. I like to see a mixture of yarns for this reason. Experiment with coarse and smooth weights of yarn to experience the different effects the textures will give you.

Another experiment to try is taking the same color and value and trying different stitches. Turn the same stitch on its side and see the difference it makes. Use the same color and a different weight yarn. Use the same color and a luminous orlon or silk.

Notice the red, white, and blue pincushions. One has a much lighter effect than the other due to the order in which the colors have been used.

Backgrounds

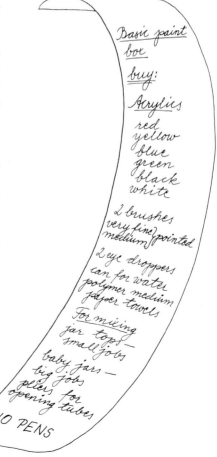

Basic paint box

buy:

Acrylics
red
yellow
blue
green
black
white

2 brushes
very fine pointed
medium pointed

2 eye droppers
can for water
polymer medium
paper towels

For mixing
jar tops —
small jobs
baby jars —
big jobs
pliers for
opening tubes

NO PENS

Although taste, discrimination, and instinct play a big part in picking out a color scheme, you also must plan your areas of color using your knowledge of repetition, contrast, and unity. You are going to have a real eyecatcher for instance, if you use red in just one area. Unless you want this for your focal point, I suggest you repeat it or soften it down. If you use full chroma it is better to use it in a smaller area and softer values in large areas. Of course, there is nothing wrong with using full primary and secondary colors on a child's chair or toy, or a modern abstract.

Try different combinations on your tracings or original designs before you put wool to canvas or material and you will save time and effort.

If you are using perspective in a landscape, be sure the strong colors are in the foreground and the greyed-out or faded colors as it stretches back to infinity. Look down a road yourself to see how true this is.

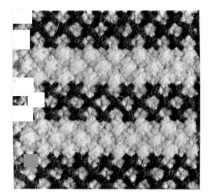

Double Straight Cross

Hungarian

Encroaching Gobelin

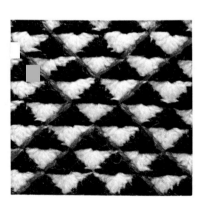

Diamond Eyelet

Byzantine

Smyrna

(top six Pictures)
Try turning your stitches in different ways and see how the light changes stitch. Next try changing top colors for combination stitches.

Long Legged Cross

Long-legged Cross Stitch may be used as a finishing stitch for coasters, clutch purses, eyeglass cases, belts, etc.

It's Indelible But It Ran

When you have finished a piece of crewel or needlepoint, put hundreds of hours of work into it, spent some good money on your materials and time on the design, it is just criminal the way some pieces turn out because proper care was not taken in washing and blocking.

How should you proceed if you purchased a kit and don't know what was used to apply the design?

For Needlepoint: Assuming there are no finishing instructions to follow, it is best to go on the assumption that it may run. You might try a test corner and if it doesn't seem to run then proceed as for Washing Your Own Designs, but if it does run here is what to do. Do not wash but dampen from the back carefully, just enough to block, and block according to instructions further on in this book.

For Material: If it is linen, it usually can be washed, but read the instructions carefully first. Wash in Woolite, rinse (both procedures should be done in cool water), roll in towel and while still damp, iron dry. You should have equipment in layers like this before ironing:

**ironing board
normal cover for board
soft terry towel
crewel face down
soft linen face towel (optional)**

Usually it is best to iron from center to outer edges. For finished pillows that are dirty, you may wash the cover and stuff it with the pillow form and extra tissue until very stretched and let dry. Do not use newspaper for stuffing as the print will come off.
The above is for finished pieces. If it is still unfinished, you may wash and block the same as needlepoint.

NEVER USE DETERGENTS OR A WASHING MACHINE.

Washing
For own designs

1. Sew up the edges either on the sewing machine or by hand. If you don't, the piece will ravel up to the finished needlepoint and then you will have nothing to block with and put your nails through. Most canvases you buy only have masking tape around them and it will come off in water.
2. Measure your work before washing.
3. Wash, using Woolite, in cool but never hot water. Swish it around until clean but do not wring out the piece but rinse thoroughly.
4. Roll in a large bath towel squeezing gently as you roll upp.
5. Proceed to blocking your needlepoint.

Blocking

Equipment Needed:
Aluminium nails or any good nails with heads on them for easy removal.
Plywood or masonite board large enough to accommodate your work.
Clean piece of muslin or other plain fabric to cover board (optional).

It is preferable to mark off your board by inches or half-inches so you get true right-angles when blocking. Be sure your material used to mark off won't bleed into needlepoint. I used india ink for making my board and then shellacked the whole board.

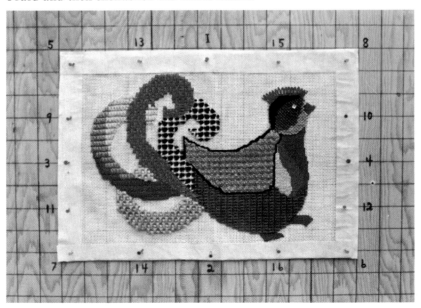

Stretch your piece back to the original size. This takes strength, sometimes of two people.

Do: place your piece FACE UP so you don't crush your stitchery. It is also easier to line up on the board this way. It should never be face down no matter what you have read in current magazines or old embroidery books. It just doesn't turn out as well.

Don't: use a staple gun for blocking as you will cut the canvas and the staples are hard to remove. Don't: put the nails through the worked canvas (the yarn) but rather through the selvage edges.

Put the nails in according to the numbers on the picture of the partridge or according to pillow diagrams. Then put secondary nails close enough between first nails to avoid a scalloped effect.

For Framed Pillow.
When blocking one through four should have tight tension, five through twelve medium tension, and thirteen through sixteen light tension so "rabbit ears" will not develop.

For Unframed Pillow.
After blocking pillow with primary nails, (numbers shown here), sew pillow according to curved line so you don't get "rabbit ears".

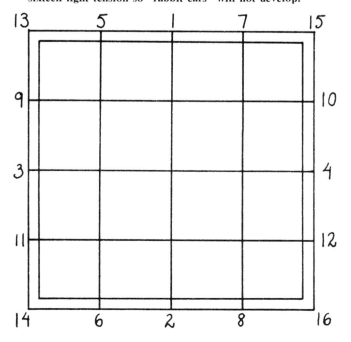

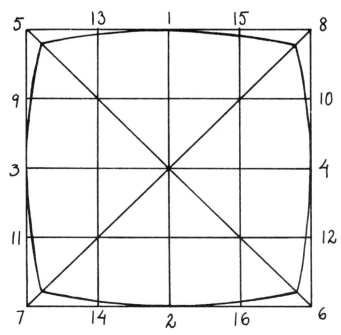

This is a very original interpretation of Marc Chagall's windows in Jerusalem. The stitcher has used a great variety of crewel stitches, padding (which was called "stump work"), appliqué, and couched gold on the Hebrew lettering. Different thicknesses of yarn and thread have been used to heighten the texture. The real windows are in different sizes but here they are all 9"×7".

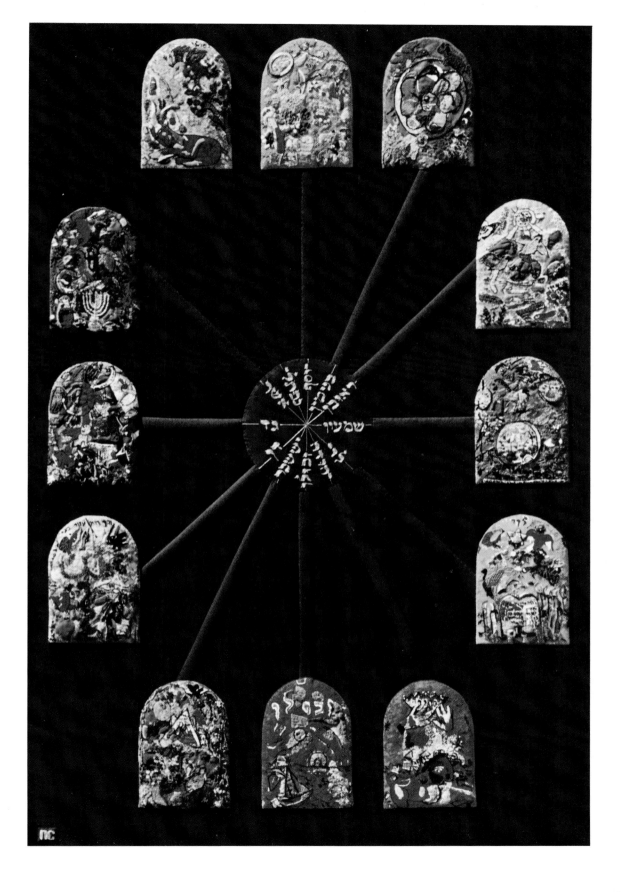

Make a cover for your musical instrument, your sporting equipment or your type-writer.

Drying

It is better to lay the board flat to dry so there is no drooping while drying.

Caution: It is not very polite to say so, but nevertheless true, that dogs and cats love wet yarn and will either urinate on it or scratch at it. Keep it high and away from them.

Be sure the piece is completely dry before removing it from the board. Usually this takes twenty-four hours. If, when you remove it, it is still out of shape, you will have to repeat the procedure of wetting and blocking until it doesn't jump back out of shape. The worst offenders are bellpulls and backgrounds which have been worked in continental tent stitch. For your own sanity, use diagonal tent or one of the other stitches for backgrounds.

On Professional Finishers

I believe that after spending your money on the best yarns and canvas or material, you should do two things to finish your work. One is to find long-wearing material to enhance your needlework.

The second is to find the best finisher you can afford, if you aren't a good seamstress yourself. After all, you have put many, many hours of work into it, and you want it to last and become an heirloom.

They should always have extra needlepoint done on them because you'll find the wool draws up after washing and even while working on the canvas. I suggest about an inch all around. Most finishers sew into the canvas work for two or three rows to be sure no unworked canvas will show.

Don't cut off unworked canvas at top and bottom until you have bought your hardware. Sometimes you may need extra canvas depending on style used.

For bellpull blocking, a good trick is to make a pocket at the bottom out of some old material, put a brick in it, pin this pocket with the brick in it on the bellpull, hang the bellpull up and let the damp bellpull block itself while drying.

In making a round piece, do not cut away unworked canvas down to two inches. It is too hard to block and finish that way. Keep the canvas square until you finish doing the work and blocking. When blocking, then, treat as a square but make it come true to circular form. After drying cut down to within one or two inches for making into finished product.

When making a rug wider than three feet, you usually have to make it in pieces to put together later as they would be too big to handle otherwise and most scrim comes thirty-six or forty inches wide.

Wash and block each piece separately before weaving together for finished product.

The hardest problem faced when sewing up a pillow is not to get "rabbit ears". This can be solved in blocking before you get to the finishing. If it has a border around it, loosen your tension at corners when you are putting in the nails. If it doesn't have a border, you may stitch on the sewing machine according to diagram on page 101.

Belts, Purses, Chairs, etc.

Bellpulls

Circular Forms

Rugs

Pillows

Color Pictures

Acknowledgements

I would like to give special and sincere thanks to all the above friends
who lent their work for this book, the men at Gullers Studio, especially
Olle Kymling and Östen Matson who worked so hard to put the book
together. Marie Almqvist did a superb job on the overlays, and Björn
Enström's stitch close ups are really great.
I also wish to thank:
Terry Hoffman who tested all the stitches and "How to Thread a
Needle."
Julie Donnelly, Bob Koch Jr., and Bill Phillips who modeled
for the book.
Mr. and Mrs. Richard William Phillips who graciously lent their house
and gardens for pictures.
Sid Garber who made the pin for the section titles from my drawings.

General Index

Light Numbers: Text
Dark Numbers: Picture

Index of Stitches

Where do I find it?

First thing I do when I'm in a strange city or town, is turn to the yellow pages of the telephone book under "Art Needlework." There you will find most of your needlepoint and crewel shops listed. Try "Embroidery" or "Needlepoint" headings next. There are over 4000 shops in the United States alone so it won't be difficult.

The large department stores have needlework sections too but not all will sell the blank canvas. This holds true of smaller shops too so it is best to call first for information on what you want to buy in the way of supplies.

When visiting other countries, try the local Embroiderers Guild for information on the best places to look, or even the textile department in the museums. Following is a partial list of suppliers, who can usually help you find good finishers too, if they don't do it themselves.

Sources of supply

United States – East

Thread Bear
127 Greenwood Ave.
Bethel, Connecticut 06801

Hook N Needle
1869 E. State Street
Westport, Connecticut 06880

Yarn and Design Studio
2156 Ponce de Leon Blvd.
Coral Gables, Florida 33134

Nantucket Needleworks
Nantucket Island
Massachusetts 02554

Needlework House
Main Street
West Townsend, Massachusetts 01474

Boutique Margot
26 W. 54th Street
New York, New York 10019

Thread Shed
307 Freeport Road
Pittsburgh, Pennsylvania 15215

Needle's Point
1626 Macon
McLean, Virginia 24503

United States – Middlewest

Swedish Knit Shop
5209 N. Clark
Chicago, Illinois 60640

Cutt Rose
1814 Central Street
Evanston, Illinois 60201

Flying Colors
9 South Lincoln
Hinsdale, Illinois

Needle Case
Farmside Country Store
Long Grove, Illinois

Wool N Wick
North Morton Ave.
Morton, Illinois 61550

Needlepoint a la carte
325 South Woodward
Birmingham, Michigan 48011

Needle Nest
431 East Lake
Wayzata, Minnesota 55391

Accent Threads
1051 Big Bend Blvd.
St Louis, Missouri 63117

United States – West

The Yarn Tree
1011 West 5th Ave.
Scottdale, Arizona 85251

Lorette's Needlepoint Studio
W. 3rd and Fairfax
Los Angeles, California 90059

Yarn Depot
545 Sutter Street
San Francisco, California 94102

Needlecraft Shop
4501 Van Nuys Blvd.
Sherman Oaks, California 91403

Thumbelina
1688 Copenhagen Drive
Solvang, California 93463

Lamprey Studio
5800 South Lewis
Tulsa, Oklahoma 74105

Arachne Webworks
2390 N.W. Thurman
Portland, Oregon

Phalice's Thread Web
West 1301 14th Ave.
Spokane, Washington 99204

Canada

Homecraft Importers
2348 West 4th Avenue
Vancouver 9, B.C.

Harmony Acres Studio
Bag 1550
St. Norbert, Manitoba ROG 2 HO

England

Needlewoman Shop
Regent Street
London W 1

Thomas Hunter
36 Northumberland Street
Newcastle 1

Francis Benjamin
4 Glentworth KStreet
London NW 1

Toye, Kenning, Spencer, Ltd.
Regalia House
Red Lion Square
London WC 1

Denmark

Handarbejdets Fremme
Bredgade 74
Kopenhagen

Eva Rosenstand
Fridbergg 23
Kopenhagen

Clara Waever
Østergade 42
Kopenhagen

Carl Permin
Ny Østerg 3
Kopenhagen

Sweden

Sisters Hultgren
Grev Turegatan 15
114 46 Stockholm

Handarbetets Vänner
Djurgårdsslätten 82—84
Stockholm

Ringvägens Varumagasin
Götgatan 96
Stockholm

Lottens Trikå
Sibyllegatan 22
Stockholm